Writers of Wales

Emyr Humphreys

Writers of Wales

Emyr Humphreys

M. Wynn Thomas

University of Wales Press

2018

British Library Cataloguing-in-Publication Data
A catalogue record for this book is available from the British Library.

ISBN 978-1-78683-296-2
e-ISBN 978-1-78683-297-9

The publisher acknowledges the financial support of the Welsh Books Council.

Typeset in Wales by Eira Fenn Gaunt, Cardiff
Printed by CPI Antony Rowe, Chippenham, Wiltshire

Contents

Prefatory Note

Some parts of the discussion that follows are heavily revised versions of materials of mine on Emyr Humphreys previously published in the following places:

Emyr Humphreys (Penygroes: Gwasg Pantycelyn, 1989).

Two essays in *Internal Difference: Twentieth-Century Writing in Wales* (Cardiff: University of Wales Press, 1992).

Chapter in *In the Shadow of the Pulpit: Literature and Nonconformist Wales* (Cardiff: University of Wales Press, 2010).

Two essays in *All That is Wales: Collected Essays* (Cardiff: University of Wales Press, 2017).

Introduction to *Conversations and Reflections* and interviews in that volume (Cardiff: University of Wales Press, 2002).

Interviews in Arwel Jones (ed.), *Dal Pen Rheswm* (Caerdydd: Gwasg Prifysgol Cymru, 1999).

Abbreviations

LK   *The Little Kingdom* (London: Eyre and Spottiswoode, 1946)

VS   *The Voice of a Stranger* (London: Eyre and Spottiswoode, 1949)

CH   *A Change of Heart* (London: Eyre and Spottiswoode, 1951)

HF   *Hear and Forgive* (London: Macdonald, 1952)

MA   *A Man's Estate* (London: Eyre and Spottiswoode, 1955)

IW   *The Italian Wife* (London: Eyre and Spottiswoode, 1957)

TE   *Y Tri Llais* (Llandybie: Llyfrau'r Dryw, 1958); *A Toy Epic* (London: Eyre and Spottiswoode, 1958)

G   *The Gift* (London: Eyre and Spottiswood, 1963)

OHB   *Outside the House of Baal* (London: Eyre and Spottiswoode, 1965)

N   *Natives* (London: Secker and Warburg, 1968)

NW   *National Winner* (London: Macdonald, 1971)

FB   *Flesh and Blood* (London: Hodder and Stoughton, 1974)

BF   *The Best of Friends* (London: Hodder and Stoughton, 1978)

AT   *The Anchor Tree* (London: Dent, 1980)

TT   *The Taliesin Tradition* (London: Black Raven Press, 1983)

J   *Jones* (London: Dent, 1984)

SE   *Salt of the Earth* (London: Dent, 1985)

AH   *An Absolute Hero* (London: Dent, 1986)

OS   *Open Secrets* (London: Dent, 1988)

BA   *Bonds of Attachment* (London: Macdonald, 1991)

US   *Unconditional Surrender* (Bridgend: Seren, 1996)

GD   *The Gift of a Daughter* (Bridgend: Seren, 1998)

CP   *Collected Poems* (Cardiff: University of Wales Press, 1999)

DPR   *Dal Pen Rheswm* (Caerdydd: Gwasg Prifysgol Cymru, 1999)

GS   *Ghosts and Strangers* (Bridgend: Seren, 2001)

CR   *Conversations and Reflections* (Cardiff: University of Wales Press, 2002)

OPP   *Old People are a Problem* (Bridgend: Seren, 2003)

S   *The Shop* (Bridgend: Seren, 2005)

WW   *The Woman at the Window* (Bridgend: Seren, 2009)

I

THE LIFE

Born in 1919, Emyr Humphreys may be usefully regarded as the last great survivor of the heroic age of twentieth-century Welsh culture. Extending roughly from the First World War to the 1970s, the period was heroic in the sense that it could boast a cohort of writers who dedicated their conspicuous talents to infusing political, as well as cultural, energy into Welsh life sufficient to arouse their country out of the long torpor of its meekly subservient position within a profoundly anglocentric 'British' polity. Humphreys shared with those earlier writers – several of whom he came to know – the view that the Welsh were as a people 'lacking that inner conviction that a free nation has of existing for its own sake'. (*CR*, 147) Exploring this psycho-cultural condition became his great undertaking as a creative writer. And his fiction may be also regarded as an attempt to ensure the self-perpetuation of a nation whose future has, virtually since its beginnings in the early post-Roman period, been continuously uncertain. But then, 'all art,' in Humphreys's view, 'is about survival.' (*CR*, 119)

The heroic age could further be broadly subdivided into two. The heroic aspects of the interwar period were largely confined to the transformative achievements of a generation of Welsh-language writer-activists of a quality unparalleled since the golden age of late medieval times. And among the culturally 'committed' of this remarkable constellation of talents one could number T. Gwynn Jones, Saunders Lewis, Kate Roberts, Ambrose Bebb, E. Tegla Davies, R. Williams Parry, W. J. Gruffydd, Gwenallt and others. While there were, by the late 1930s, some stirrings of like political energy among some of the young anglophone writers of the Dylan Thomas generation centred on the maverick periodical *Wales* and its editor, the wayward and wilful ringmaster of talent, Keidrych Rhys, it was not until the 1960s that a grouping of English-language writers emerged steadily animated by a liberationist political passion.

As for the heroic politico-cultural commitments of the transitional period between the Second World War and the 1960s, they were almost exclusively the preserve of two giant talents: R. S. Thomas and his friend and companion-in-arms Emyr Humphreys. Anglophone writers both, they nevertheless deliberately identified themselves with the important Welsh-language figures of the previous generation, and took as mentor and guru the greatest of these, Saunders Lewis, remarkable for his creative talents, his controversial ideological genius, his charismatic personality and his fearless political activism.[1] Of all the 'heroic' writers considered above it could be said, in Lewis's words, that

> What these writers and poets have in common is an awareness that the Welsh nation may be dying of indifference and sloth and that a literature of a thousand years may end with a whimper. In that they have, as it were, an epitome of what now overhangs all Europe, of what threatens humanity, a destruction of civilization through apathy.[2]

Thomas and Humphreys alike could be not inappropriately styled 'the sons of Saunders'. Not that Humphreys's views could be comfortably conflated with those of Lewis. He has always been a much more staunch and ardent advocate of Wales's Nonconformist heritage than Lewis, the Catholic convert who (despite, or because of, being the son of a prominent Welsh Calvinistic minister) was ever tart of tongue on the subject. And while both were ardent Europhiles, it is to Germany and Italy that Humphreys looks for examples of European culture at its richest, while Lewis was besotted with the imperious culture of France, like his own hero, the nineteenth-century controversialist and visionary cultural nationalist Emrys ap Iwan.

But while Humphreys has always emphasised the social role of the Welsh writer, he has not been unaware of the perils and tensions associated with a writer's attempt to serve her or his community by active and practical cultural interventions. It was Saunders Lewis, after all, who – with more than half an eye to his own case – warned the young R. S. Thomas to take seriously Yeats's admonition to young writers to aim either at 'perfection of the life', or at 'perfection of the art': to attempt both was likely to lead only to creative suicide. And Humphreys himself is on record as stating that so many of the great figures of the remarkable generation of talent that inexplicably appeared in Wales during the first half of the twentieth century had, in the end, for all their brilliance, somewhat underachieved as writers because too much of their creative energies had been self-sacrificingly deflected into cultural and political activities of vital importance to the survival of their people. 'How was poor old Kate Roberts going to find time to write lengthy novels,' he poignantly enquires, naming one of the most distinguished short story writers not only of Wales but of Europe, 'while she was killing herself keeping *Y Faner* [Wales's leading Welsh-language weekly] going?' (*DPR*, 120)

He has continued to believe that twentieth-century Welsh-language writing, at its best, can provide anglophone writers of Wales, such as himself, with both inspiration and resource, and 'protect them from the dangers of self-conscious provincialism'. Accordingly, he has urged any English-language author to

immerse him- or herself in the intellectual vision of Saunders Lewis, the zeal and eloquence of Ambrose Bebb, the analytical honesty of Kate Roberts, the idiomatic strength of W. J. Gruffydd, the urbane sophisticated narrative of R. T. Jenkins, the moral integrity of Lewis Valentine. (*CR*, 222)

Like that of such writers as these, most of Emyr Humphreys's own work is intensely concerned to address the 'condition of Wales', although always within a pan-European perspective: but 'to be more European', he has prophetically observed, 'we need first to be more Welsh.' (*CR*, 149) The discussion that follows will therefore necessarily concentrate on those aspects of his writing that relate to this central preoccupation, and will primarily confine itself to the fiction. There will be no discussion of his work for television, both in Welsh and English. And the text will begin with a preliminary mapping of the mental world of an author who has, in some respects, accomplished for twentieth-century Wales what William Faulkner accomplished for his South by devising Yoknapatawpha County: created a whole, compelling 'parallel reality', an imaginary country, abiding reference to which as a kind of 'control', I would venture to suggest, is likely to prove of substantial benefit both to Welsh readers and to others interested in Wales even today. It makes him a 'necessary figure', to employ the phrase he himself used to describe Saunders Lewis.[3]

* * *

'Where were you when you were fifteen?'
The question puzzled me. Why should he ask and damn it why should he ask . . .
'In a school', I said, 'In North-East Wales.'
Lars laughed, but I didn't mean it as a joke.
'That's funny the way you divide up Wales. Does anybody else do it but you?' (G, 19)

Wales is such a tiny country, to outsiders it often seems a single, monocellular entity. But Emyr Humphreys has always known otherwise. He has accordingly devoted much of his fiction to mapping the inner cultural and historical complexity of this small peninsula to the far west of England whose people have so stubbornly persisted, against considerable odds, in accounting themselves a nation. And in the process he has repeatedly drawn attention to the frequently neglected border region where he was himself born and raised.

'I was brought up', says Michael in the opening sentence of *A Toy Epic* (1958), 'in a broad valley in one of the four corners of Wales.' (*TE*, 17) And so was Humphreys. His father was headmaster of the Church School in Trelawnyd (then Newmarket), Flintshire, a stone's throw from the English border and inland from the popular, populous, increasingly anglicised coastal resort of Rhyl.[4] Indeed, the 'peculiar' circumstances of his early environment were to strike Humphreys in later life as invaluable from the perspective of a creative writer. It was more socially diverse than might be supposed, with the miners from the 'Parlwr Du' ('Point of Ayr') colliery rubbing shoulders with the farming community to which his mother's extensive family belonged – Humphreys has accordingly taken an interest in farming life throughout his life. And the coastal settlements of Rhyl and Prestatyn were already burgeoning into the anglicised fairgrounds and pleasure gardens of the Lancashire working class.

As for his immediate family, before training to be a teacher his father had grown up in Ffestiniog, son of a worker in the great slate quarries of that district. Yet although his had been a thoroughly Welsh-speaking background he had opted to anglicise himself pretty thoroughly, his conversion from Nonconformity to Anglicanism being part of his preparation to become a devoted servant of the British Empire in the alien distant outpost of Trelawnyd. The proud possessor during the 1930s of the only wireless in the village, he was wont to post BBC news bulletins on a noticeboard for the edification of the natives. By nature quiet and mild, he had been rendered permanently irritable by the chronic after-effects of gassing during the First World War, in which he had volunteered for service despite being otherwise exempt as a schoolmaster. Humphreys's mother was of a contrary nature, mercurial and rebellious whereas her husband was cautiously conformist and conservative. She would sneak out, without her husband's knowledge, for a quiet smoke and would take off periodically on jaunts to enjoy the exciting jollities of the seaside towns. Humphreys has repeatedly modelled his spirited and independent-minded female characters on that of his mother, most notably perhaps that of Lydia in *Outside the House of Baal* (1965).

While Emyr was their only son, he was not the first child to share their hearth. When Mrs Humphreys's twin sister died in childbirth the pair adopted the tiny baby, several years before Emyr's arrival. And John Elwyn grew up to become every bit as stoutly Tory and piously Anglican as his adoptive father had been. Ordained as priest in the Church in Wales following training at Llandaff, he ended his days as an Anglican canon ministering to the spiritual needs of ex-pat Brits sunning themselves in the Algarve and nearby Escoril. Despite the radical difference in their careers, Emyr Humphreys and his brother remained close friends right up to the latter's death. And of course, while John Elwyn faithfully emulated his father, Emyr could be said to have rebelled against him in every important particular. Although passingly attracted to High Anglicanism in his youth, and even briefly contemplating taking holy orders in the Church in Wales, he eventually chose to throw in his spiritual lot with the Annibynwyr (roughly the 'Welsh Independents', or 'Congregationalists'), the denomination to which his wife belonged, and from which his father had converted to Anglicanism, having been disillusioned with Nonconformist chaplains in the Army during the Great War. It was also the denomination in which his gentle and godly father-in-law (who lived with them for sixteen years after their marriage) had served as minister throughout his life. The Annibynwyr were a denomination peculiarly suited to Humphreys's principled and highly individualistic nature since they placed such a high premium on individual conscience and personal liberty.

His attachment to the Annibynwyr was undoubtedly reinforced by his important friendship with R. Tudur Jones. They had been contemporaries at Rhyl County School, but became close friends only years later, by which time Jones was not only a highly respected minister with the Annibynwyr but a distinguished Professor of Church History, a combative conservative (Calvinist) theologian, the definitive historian of Wales's Nonconformist culture, and a trenchant advocate, through his newspaper columns, of Welsh nationhood and of the importance of the Welsh language. Already a towering figure on the Welsh Nonconformist stage, he went on to enjoy a global reputation as worldwide President of the Confederation of Congregational Churches – a denomination particularly strong in the US ever since the time of the founding fathers. Jones's influence on Humphreys's thinking remains to be carefully considered by future scholars.[5]

There were also unusual features to Humphreys's natal landscape. He and his brother, for example, spent considerable time in the company of the local Rector, a native of Cardiganshire turned 'Oxford' man, his pride in such being both ridiculous and endearing. His unmarried sister likewise had acquired considerable social pretensions. As for Humphreys's playground as a child, it was Clip y Gop, the prehistoric man-made hill that rose behind Trelawnyd. From the top of Y Gop, the great city of Liverpool beckoned invitingly to the east, while Snowdonia loomed in majestic profile to the west: Dixie Dean (his parents were passionate Everton supporters) or Llywelyn Fawr, which was it to be? As a borderer, the young Humphreys soon became aware of a choice between orientating himself in the one direction or the other.

For him, the decisive turn came when attending the sixth form at Rhyl County School. From one of his teachers, Moses Jones, he learned of the recent protest-burning by a small group of Welsh Nationalists led by Saunders Lewis of the training school for bombers the Westminster government had insisted, in the teeth of Wales-wide protests, on building at what had been the site of Penyberth, a historic old farmhouse on the Llŷn peninsula. The fire lit there in 1936, and the imprisonments that followed, kindled his imagination.[6] Its light showed him Wales to be a colonised nation and the whole of his long writing career has primarily involved a creative exploration of the implications of that subordinated and subservient condition. Likewise, his principled attempts to instigate a process of decolonisation began when in his youth he became involved in a campaign to have the name of his natal village changed back from Newmarket to Trelawnyd. And since the most damaged victim of colonisation had, he discovered, been the Welsh language and its culture, he began to learn Welsh as a late teenager, eventually adopting it as his first language. Penyberth was his first introduction to the thinking of Saunders Lewis – also a borderer, born in Wallasey on the Wirral – on whose view of Wales and its place in the wider world Humphreys was to model his own throughout his career. While he had been introduced to Lewis's work by Moses Jones, he was not to meet

Saunders Lewis until 1938, when their paths crossed at a Plaid Cymru meeting.

Despite his deep commitment to the Welsh language and its culture – which he regards as the irreplaceable core of a continuing Welsh identity – Humphreys has (like his close friend R. S. Thomas) never felt sufficiently inward with it to feel comfortable producing creative work in Welsh. And, again like Thomas, he has written feelingfully about his dilemma:

> If you object to globalisation you must flourish in the local root; and the local root is the language that belongs to the landscape; and the language that belongs to the landscape here in Wales is Welsh. That is the theorem on which I base my work, and it enables me to understand the agony of a Jewish poet like Paul Celan, who was writing in German. It is, for the artist, a suicidal situation, a situation which in Celan's case resulted in actual physical suicide.[7] One of the escape routes is fiction, because story is a language of its own, a music of its own, a supranational language which is detached from the cultural problem. And that may be one reason why, culturally situated as I am, I find fiction such a very attractive form. (*CR*, 131)

Elsewhere, he has further noted 'that the ace that the bilingual novelist has in hand is his ancestral language . . . Two languages should make a writer more aware of the complexities of a multi-lingual world.' (*CR*, 221)

Even though he has long been completely and impressively fluent in Welsh and has chosen to live most of his life entirely through that second language, English has always been Emyr Humphreys's preferred medium for writing poems and novels. Plays, however, have been a different matter, as many of them were commissioned for televising by S4C, following its establishment on 1 November 1982 as a separate, Welsh-only, channel. They were therefore inevitably written entirely in Welsh. Otherwise, his Welsh-language output has been confined to the early novella *Y Tri Llais* (1958) (the product of special circumstances during his time at the BBC, as we shall see, and enabled by the fact that at that time his father-in-law, a reliable Welsh scholar, was living in the Humphreys family home at Penarth) and some poems written in his old age.

Nevertheless, learning Welsh was a turning point both in his personal life and in his creative development. It had enabled him, he later felt, to read a geographical and cultural landscape that previously had been illegible. It afforded him access to the deep time of Welsh history buried – just like the ancient Welsh princess reputed to lie beneath the prehistoric burial mound of Y Gop – below the surface of contemporary life, and inaccessible to his monoglot English compatriots. In due course, his fiction, too, became dedicated partly to the work of disclosing this hidden Wales to itself – although he has always regarded the impulse to write as first and foremost a personal compulsion rather than an act of social, cultural or political commitment, emphasising that fundamental to his writer's nature is to view life as a source of raw material for fiction. However, given his longstanding concern, as a writer, to address the history of Wales, it was appropriate that he chose to pursue the study of History to degree level at the University College of Wales, Aberystwyth. In choosing this subject and determining to study it at Aberystwyth he had been influenced by T. I. Ellis, his headmaster at Rhyl County School, who was the son of the legendary Liberal politician T. E. Ellis and consequently obliged to suffer the sobriquet 'mab y monument' ('the son of the monument') following the erection of a statue in Bala to commemorate his famous father. Ellis was also an enthusiastic arranger of summer camps for boys and Humphreys benefited from them. This enthusiasm of Ellis's for camping was shared by another teacher, P. H. Burton, future mentor of Richard Burton of course, whom Humphreys accordingly met during this schoolboy period.

He has always insisted that he was a very poor scholar at school until he reached the sixth form. (In those days, two years of study in the sixth – which was optional – was a preparation for sitting testing exams with a view to university entry.) Then he seemed to come alive, but continued to be stimulated as much by extra-curricular reading as by his formal course of study. Rhyl Public

Library, in particular, became his favourite destination on a Saturday, and it was there that he read his way through some of the work of T. S. Eliot and James Joyce – both of whom became early heroes of his – and encountered in the pages of the popular *GK's Weekly* the Distributist economic theories that were much in vogue at that time. By the end of his period in the sixth form he was seriously considering training for the Anglican priesthood – unbeknownst to his parents he had even secretly visited a Catholic priest for information about the Catholic Church – and it was as a first step in that direction that he opted for graduate study at the University College of Wales, Aberystwyth.

He entered college in 1937, and during his period of study there found that the student body (then numbering no more than some six hundred in total) was becoming more and more polarised between red-hot Socialists and impassioned Welsh Nationalists. While he was already primed to identify with the latter, among the luminaries of the former persuasion were talented individuals such as Glanmor Williams (later a renowned historian of Wales) and the shy, glamorous young postgraduate Alun Lewis, already the cynosure of girls' eyes. Humphreys shared a house with a leading young Labour activist, Emyr Currie Jones, to whom he was to remain close throughout the latter's life, including the period when he became one of the most influential Labour figures on Cardiff City Council.

Their informal fiery debates found a more formal outlet in the context of the Debating Society of which Humphreys was a member, and in due course many of his novels were to be structured along the lines of ideological debate. So committed a Nationalist was he already that he served for a period as the Secretary of the student branch of Plaid Cymru. He was also active in the Celtic Society, the body devoted to promotion of Welsh-language literature. Dominated by aspiring poets, it showed little interest in other cultural forms. Nevertheless, Humphreys did develop an interest in Continental film, viewing the work of great directors such as Eisenstein, Pudovkin, Dreyer, Buñuel and Pabst in the little cinema on the pier. Many years later he was to discover and admire the work of Ingmar Bergman.

Another fundamental division within the student community grew as war loomed, with some preparing to serve in the forces while others, of like number and sympathetic to the pacifist movements already strong among the Left and among Welsh Nonconformist denominations, were already determined to register as conscientious objectors. The coming of war interrupted Humphreys's degree studies and also brought an end to his brief intention to enter holy orders with the Anglican Church.

But his most important education at this time came not from classroom study but through the close friendship he formed with the prodigiously knowledgeable D. Myrddin Lloyd, with whom he shared student digs. Ten years older than his friend, Lloyd was already an outstanding established scholar not only of Old Welsh literature but also of Old Irish Literature, as well as being steeped in the history of Wales and consumed by a passion for French literature. Like Humphreys, Lloyd was a confirmed, impassioned nationalist and perfectly equipped to provide Humphreys's nationalism with sound underpinnings in the history both of Welsh and Continental culture. Having just returned from perfecting his Gaelic at the then National University of Ireland, Lloyd had been newly appointed Assistant in the Department of Printed Books at the National Library of Wales and was to spend the final years of his distinguished career as keeper of printed books at the National Library of Scotland. An incomparable raconteur and magical conjurer of the romance of the past, he enchanted the imagination of the young Humphreys, while also opening his eyes to the European dimension of Welsh cultural history of which Saunders Lewis was already at that time making so much.[8]

On the outbreak of war, Humphreys – whose abhorrence of war had long been incubating as he watched his father dealing with the debilitating after-effects of his gassing in the trenches and who was already actively involved with the Peace Pledge Union – registered as a conscientious objector and non-combatant on both religious and nationalist grounds. He spent a few enjoyable years working on the land, briefly in Pembrokeshire and then (from 1941) at Llanfaglan near Caernarfon, before repairing to London in

1943 for training with the Save the Children Fund. During that period he shared a house in Chelsea packed with books with Basil MacTaggart, a slightly older man whose long experience of living on the Continent had made him a sophisticated, multilingual European and who was to become his lifelong friend.

Under MacTaggart's tutelage, Humphreys began to learn French and German. It was another crucial phase in his cultural and political education. Next came service in Egypt (a period that saw him visit Palestine and Jerusalem), before he followed the northern progress of the invading Allied armies up through Italy, where at war's end he helped run a large refugee centre catering for some 7,000 people in the Florence area with MacTaggart. He accordingly became fluent in Italian and a devotee of the life and culture of Italy. At the same time, his devotion to Wales was steadily reinforced by his reading of the brilliantly original comments on contemporary affairs, viewed from a challengingly unorthodox Welsh perspective, supplied by Saunders Lewis, under the title 'Cwrs y Byd' ('World Affairs'), to the Welsh weekly paper *Y Faner*, a copy of which was regularly sent to Humphreys throughout his period in wartime service. 'While you are privileged with a little solitude in your sweaty sleeping quarters in the Administration block,' he later wrote of his time in Florence, 'you read successive numbers of "Cwrs y Byd" . . . far into the hot night.' (*CR*, 86)

His experience in Italy made him a convinced Welsh European and a novelist who has consistently situated himself within the European literary tradition. This is hardly surprising given the extraordinary opportunities he was afforded in this phase of his life. For example, he wistfully recalls lying on his back for an hour surveying Michelangelo's great ceiling in an otherwise totally deserted Sistine Chapel. And the Florentine camp was located in the very heart of the medieval city, allowing him easy access to all its great cultural treasures. As for the uprooted condition of the refugees themselves, it permanently underlined for him the complex necessities of an intimate attachment to place, faced as he was with Italian peasants desperate to return to their land in Abruzzo. But it also brought him into intimate contact with Jewish refugees from

Central Europe equally desperate to emigrate to a totally new life in Palestine. Rootedness on the one hand, a deep desire for the freedom to escape to a new country and into a new selfhood on the other: his fiction was eventually to explore both impulses with equal understanding and sympathy. One brief outcome of his period in post-war Italy was a respect for the Communist Party – the most efficient by far of those that were at that time trying to rebuild the country. As for the Welsh Europeanism born of his wartime experiences, that was accidentally reflected in the international circumstances surrounding the publication of his first novel, *The Little Kingdom*, in 1946. Although it was published only after his return to Britain, it had actually been composed during the period he spent working in Egypt.

Humphreys's Welsh Europeanism has always been firmly centred in his beloved Italy. For him, it is 'the home of European culture as a whole – the source of Latin, the source of medieval civilization'. (*CR*, 134) During the time he spent there, he got to know Vittorini, and came to admire Sciascia, the Sicilian writer, while Montale and Ungaretti became important to him. 'Pirandello and Verga,' he has noted, 'are modern writers of the novella tradition that stretches back to Boccaccio.'[9] And Dante, above all others, has been one of the major presences throughout his life. He confesses to a love of *paese* – the equivalent of *brogarwch* ('attachment to locality') that makes Italy, like Wales, a 'continent not a country . . . that includes an infinite number of regional variations and local dialects'. (*CR*, 134) Above all, he can identify with Italy because, like Wales – and like modern Germany, he interestingly adds – it is a 'defeated nation', its nationalism chastened accordingly. Humphreys strongly approves of that, contrasting such an attitude to the swagger of the *soi-disant* 'undefeated' French.[10]

Maturing into an adult during the 1930s – that grim decade of class struggle, economic depression and monstrous totalitarian ideologies – had left its mark permanently on the mind of a young man who had been born into the immediate aftermath of the Great War that had left his father's health and temperament permanently damaged. Consequently, much of his fiction was to be concerned with the ethical dilemmas that were the residue of his youthful experiences. On the one hand, for instance, he embraced a pacifism rooted in a visceral objection to the culture of international violence of whose destructive consequences he'd had early experience in his father's crippled state – a notable feature of his novels is their repeated depiction of psychologically impaired and accordingly 'weakened' male characters. On the other hand, he knew that such cultural and political independence as he profoundly wished for his Wales had historically been achieved by small colonised nations only through violent freedom struggles. The creative inner tensions generated by such dualities were to incline him to structure his fiction along the lines of debate and dialectic, and to weave a complex narrative web of ambiguities and ambivalences.

Two years after war's end Humphreys returned to Wales to marry the daughter of a gentle minister who was to become, for the last sixteen years of life, a beloved member of the family and who in the process allowed Humphreys extensive intimate insight into Nonconformist Wales. Elinor Humphreys's contribution to his life and career in writing deserves not only special mention but extensive consideration. As well as being wife and mother (to four children: Dewi, Mair, Sion and Robin), she functioned in effect as a creative collaborator, acting as his first, and most critical, reader, and undertaking the process of turning manuscript into typescript preparatory to publication. Humphreys had first met her when he was working on the land at Llanfaglan and teaching night-classes for the WEA. At that time, she was still a schoolgirl, living at home in Bontnewydd. Their relationship blossomed during the period Humphreys spent training with the Save the Children Fund in London, where Elinor was by then a young nurse. Although he had lived in the capital through the dread period of the flying bombs, Humphreys was to look back on this period as an idyllic one.

It was his complete devotion to Elinor that brought Humphreys back to Wales at the end of his period of service with the Save the Children Fund, despite the powerful attraction to him by that time of a Continental life-style. They were married immediately upon

Humphreys's return from Italy, and spent a period living in Llan-fyllin (near Bala), while he worked for several youth organisations and was visited for the first time by a rather gauche young clergy-man poet named R. S. Thomas who was also beginning to find his way as an aspiring writer and who turned up squashed into a tiny car being driven by the flamboyant Keidrych Rhys.[11] It was the beginning of a warm friendship between poet and novelist that lasted a lifetime. He next completed a teachers' training course at University College Bangor that led in 1948 to two crucially formative years teaching at Wimbledon Technical College.

During that time in London he greatly enjoyed the stimulating company in the Chelsea area of a glamorous galaxy of young writers and artists, talents both established and emergent, excited by the promise of a post-war world and the social revolution being engineered by the Attlee Labour government. The theatre was a ready attraction, and he enjoyed lunching at the Garrick or the Saville. He mixed with luminaries such as John Betjeman while also forming an acquaintance with Rosamund Lehmann and a friendship with Pamela Hansford Johnson warm enough to receive an invitation to her marriage to C. P. Snow. His neighbours included T. S. Eliot and the Anthony Powell who was embarking on *A Dance to the Music of Time*. A young Huw Wheldon was another he came to know, and to admire despite his very different view of Wales and of the Welsh language. Humphreys took to frequenting the London theatre (Shakespearean parallels were to underpin several of the plots of his early novels), and made the acquaintance of that very famous product of his native district, the actor and author Emlyn Williams, with whom he was later to work. It was the golden age of Tyrone Guthrie and such giants of the English stage as Laurence Olivier (whom Humphreys saw performing Mr Puff in Sheridan's *The Critics* and *Oedipus Rex* on the same night), John Gielgud, Edith Evans and Ralph Richardson. New talents such as Bertolt Brecht and Samuel Beckett were just beginning to make their mark.

The National Gallery was another attraction, and among the contemporary painters known personally to him was Patrick Heron, with whom he also formed a lasting friendship, while a particularly important admirer at this early juncture was Graham Greene, who had already spotted Humphreys's gifts as a fiction writer and was a valued early mentor. Greene it was who, when working as literary editor of *The Spectator*, had first read a manuscript, in the form of a fictional autobiography, sent him in 1943 by the young Humphreys who had mistakenly believed the editor was still his fellow-Welshman Goronwy Rees. Having been heavily revised and reworked, this originally callow first text (that had begun life as a poetic narrative) was more than a dozen years later to form the basis of his early prize-winning novella *A Toy Epic*.[12] Much taken with the potential of the manuscript, Greene urged it be expanded, only to reject it in its re-presented form as being now too diffused and unfocused. Despite this rebuff, Humphreys continued to maintain a close contact with his mentor.

But although Greene strongly urged him to remain in London and cultivate his growing metropolitan connections, Humphreys decided to move his family back to Wales in 1951 so that the children could be raised in a Welsh-speaking culture. Several years of teaching followed at the grammar school in Pwllheli, a coastal town on the north-west peninsula of Llŷn that eventually came to be represented as 'Pendraw' in his *Land of the Living* sequence of novels. During this time he formed a fruitful collaborative friendship with 'Wil Sam', W. S. Jones, a brilliant unorthodox creator of 'local' plays in a highly original and distinctively Welsh Surrealist style. Together they established a small experimental theatre called 'Y Gegin' ('the Kitchen').[13] Receipt of the Somerset Maugham award for his fourth published novel *Hear and Forgive* (1952) entailed spending a period on the Continent, and so Humphreys decamped with his family first for Klagenfurt, a Carinthian town of particular interest to him as a border writer because it is in a region of Austria that is very near the Slovenian border. The family next proceeded to the 'Salzburg seminar' in Leopoldskran that brought him into contact with a number of prominent cultural figures of the day, most notably Edmund Wilson.[14] Having had an enticing taste of life beyond the schoolroom, he returned home in 1955 not to Pwllheli but to an appointment as producer first of radio drama and later of television drama for BBC Wales in Cardiff.

Primitive, compared to later decades, though the production technology of the period was (Humphreys has emphasised the problems presented by cameras limited in number and anchored *in situ*, as well as by the expectation that plays be shot without a single break), the 1950s were a golden age in the development at Cardiff of a semi-independent broadcasting service. It was staffed by visionary figures such as Hywel Davies, Lorraine Davies, May Jones, Aneirin Talfan Davies and others of their remarkable calibre. Several of these were children of the manse, like Reith himself, and accordingly shared his high-minded view of the BBC as an institution ideally placed to educate, as well as to entertain, the public. They were also figures steeped in what might be called 'traditional' Welsh culture and determined in particular to bring not only the work of great figures of the past but also exciting figures of the Welsh present to wider public notice. Additionally, their missionary zeal extended to commissioning new creative work for broadcasting. During his ten heady years at the BBC, working first in radio and then also in television, Humphreys duly commissioned new material and pioneered a series of Welsh translations of contemporary European drama, inspired to do so in part by his friendship with Martin Esslin.[15] The Theatre of the Absurd was a particular interest, and among the works that resulted were Saunders Lewis's translation of *Waiting for Godot*, and other translations of plays by Dürrenmatt and Brecht.

At this time, he worked with a number of notable writers and actors, including Kenneth Griffith, Emlyn Williams, Hugh Griffith, Clifford Evans, and the young star trio of Siân Phillips, Richard Burton and Peter O'Toole. Particularly important to him was the extremely close and fruitful working friendship he developed with the elderly Saunders Lewis. Although their paths had previously crossed so infrequently that he was virtually unknown to Lewis, first a meeting engineered by Humphreys at the Park Hotel, and subsequently their neighbourliness in Penarth meant the two came into increasingly close personal contact. They established a tradition of meeting weekly for lunch, and Humphreys not only produced plays such as *Siwan, Gymerwch chi Sigaret?*, *Brad* and *Esther* for broadcasting, he also arranged for them to be translated into English both for radio and for television production.

Another major Welsh dramatist with whom he worked closely was John Gwilym Jones, who, unlike Lewis, was not only a close friend but also Humphreys's contemporary, and a rising talent of the Welsh stage.[16] They were to collaborate fruitfully again later at Bangor. The notable plays by Jones that Humphreys produced in both Welsh and English for broadcasting were *Y Tad a'r Mab*, *Y Gŵr Llonydd*, *Lle Mynno'r Gwynt*, *Barcud yn Farcud Fyth*, and *Pry Ffenest*. Having already published four widely acclaimed novels before joining the Corporation, he somehow managed to publish another four while working for the BBC. One of these, *A Toy Epic*, a fictionalised version of a radio play he had himself written and produced for the BBC, won the prestigious Hawthornden Prize in 1958, while another, *Outside the House of Baal*, is widely regarded as the best anglophone novel of the twentieth century in Wales.

His period working in drama also left its mark on his subsequent work as a novelist. In particular it encouraged him to build novels out of a series of short, condensed theatrical scenes, a practice also influenced by his interest in the blocks of colour in the abstract paintings of such distinguished modern artists as Patrick Heron, who during his Chelsea days had introduced him to Terry Frost and Roger Hilton. Exposure to European drama had kindled an interest, thanks partly to his acquaintance with Martin Esslin, in Brechtian *Verfremdungseffekt*, a revolutionary theory at the time that was reflected in his growing fictional practice of neutral presentation of both characters and action. Working through the medium of Welsh had intensified his concern to use a stripped-back English, designed to avoid any suggestion of the overwriting for which (following the successes of Dylan Thomas and Gwyn Thomas) the Anglo-Welsh had become notorious. And the development of such a minimalist style enabled him to mediate Welsh-language experience through English without any of the quaint or grotesque distortions that writers such as Caradoc Evans had so infamously favoured.

The constant drain of his BBC work on the creative energies he needed to reserve for writing fiction prompted Humphreys to leave the corporation in 1965 to establish a Drama Department at the University College of North Wales, Bangor. Having expected to be based within the Welsh Department, he was deeply disappointed to discover that his base was now in the Department of English. He was also disappointed in the hope that he would find ample time for writing during his period in post – in the event, the only fiction he managed to produce was *Natives* (1968) and *National Winner* (1971). But his period at Bangor sharpened his sense of the vital importance for the Welsh language to have full access to the modern media, and it deepened his conviction that the medium itself needed as much careful attention as the content, since it was the medium that was the message. His emphasis as an academic, therefore, was on teaching his students how to 'read' the media, although during the college holidays he did work informally with the students on productions of plays by both Saunders Lewis and his close friend and colleague at Bangor, John Gwilym Jones.

After seven years in post he resigned to devote his time entirely to his own writing, and the next fifty years saw the publication of some two dozen further novels, novellas and short-story collections, including the epic seven-novel *Land of the Living* sequence (1971–91), as well as the completion of a very substantial body of poetry. In addition, he published a remarkable work of cultural history, *The Taliesin Tradition* (1983), which argued for the central role played over almost two millennia by writers (traditionally the tribal poets or bards) and related shape-shifters in the maintenance of a stubborn but resourcefully fluid Welsh national identity totally unsupported by any legal or political structure. It was a work as revealing of his sense of his own cultural responsibilities as were the powerful essays on civic, political and cultural affairs (duly collected in *Conversations and Reflections*, 2002) he produced in his role as a concerned and committed public intellectual not averse to direct practical intervention in national affairs.

During the 1960s and early 1970s Humphreys had been an active dissenter himself, having refused to pay for a monolingual television licence and having also declined to complete the 1971 census form because it had so contemptuously ignored the Welsh language. The former action led to a week's imprisonment in Walton gaol in Liverpool in May, 1973 – he was spared a longer term thanks to a warder discovering a sum in his trouser pocket sufficient to cover the licence fee he had been refusing to pay. Eventually Humphreys was to prove a leading figure in the campaign, mounted by *Cymdeithas Yr Iaith Gymraeg/Welsh Language Society*, to establish a separate Welsh-language television channel.

The tradition of dissent was therefore naturally one of the subjects that moved him to script and produce a number of television features during the 1970s and early 1980s for commercial television in Wales. A few of these – most notably studies of Kate Roberts and of the *Mabinogion*, and a seven-programme series on Great Dissenters (*Y Gwrthwynebwyr*, 1973) that placed the Welsh Puritan martyr of Elizabethan times John Penry in the company of Lenin and Dietrich Bonhoeffer – took the form of drama-documentaries for HTV and for Channel Four. He also produced documentary studies of the history of the Welsh in America screened in 1974 as *Y Baradwys Bell/Our American Dream*. The establishment at the beginning of that decade of the groundbreaking Welsh-language television channel S4C, for which he had long selflessly campaigned, also afforded him a new opportunity to write drama scripts for peak-hour screening, resulting in the production of some twenty original Welsh-language plays for television. An invaluable collaborator in this work was his second son, Sion, a talented film director – his eldest son, Dewi, having opted for a mainstream career in London as director of such series as *The Vicar of Dibley* and *Open All Hours*.

Humphreys's work on Dissenters, in particular, emphasised his awareness of operating in a European context. From the very beginning, he had perceived that the centuries-old Welsh experience of living in the threatening shadow first of England and then of an increasingly global and overwhelmingly powerful anglo-american culture meant that the 'Welsh condition' which was his own immediate concern as an author was also a condition genuinely representative of the majority of peoples and cultures throughout the modern world. And one consequence of this abiding awareness of the international dimension of the Welsh case was the attention he paid, as an avowed 'Welsh European', to the intersection of Welsh and Continental affairs in many of his late novels.

2

PREOCCUPATIONS

Humphreys's writing has always drawn extensively on the breadth of experiences and familiarity with different localities and cultures afforded by his varied working life. The early London novel *Hear and Forgive*, for example, offers sharp vignettes of the edgy, bitchy, competitive relations that the claustrophobic atmosphere of a school staffroom can so readily encourage, and *The Gift* (1963), another early work, accurately and sympathetically captures the uneasy, unstable mix of arrogance and uncertainty that is an actor's ego. Humphreys's lifelong love of Italy informs novels such as *The Italian Wife* (1957), while *The Voice of a Stranger* (1949) draws on his initial exposure at the refugee transit camp to the country in its anarchic immediate post-war state when all social order had collapsed along with traditional values.

In this murky post-war milieu of murderous political man-oeuvrings and duplicitous human relations a young Welshman, well-meaning to the point of culpable innocence, finds himself morally compromised. It is one of the earliest examples of Humphreys grappling with what became a central preoccupation. The generative tension in his mind between an attraction to the progressive theology and liberal ethics of twentieth-century Welsh Nonconformity, and Saunders Lewis's sternly minatory insistence that what was best in the Welsh religious and literary tradition had always been stiffened by an unbending Calvinist awareness of original sin. A journal entry of this period offers us a window onto his state of mind:

One begins to believe that honesty doesn't exist outside the imagination and that selfishness is the hand and brain of life. It needs an Elizabethan to do justice to Europe today, another Webster. For we are too much like cold fish caught in a net swivelling an eye over the expiring species.[1]

And like Webster, Humphreys did not scruple to use devices of melodrama in his novels to convey the ferocity of the moral struggle that underlies the calm surface of ordinary life. In addition to several murders, his fiction has touched on other lurid human practices, including incest. But in the face of his early acquaintance in the Florentine camp with human frailties, he has always resolutely refused to discount the mystery of human goodness, even though there is scarcely an instance of such in his fiction that is entirely unambiguous. Indeed, some of his greatest creations – most notably the central character of the aged minister J.T. in *Outside the House of Baal* – are compelling precisely because their moral character remains, in the final analysis, so stubbornly indeterminate in nature. Time after time he is drawn back to such enigmas.

'I developed in Florence the "balcony attitude to life",' Humphreys later wrote, 'the penalty of being a pilgrim in a foreign land, no doubt.'[2] Fleetingly he contemplated staying in Italy, free from all the sentimental ties and moral obligations inescapably attendant upon a post-war return to Wales. But return he did, to a career of total commitment to the politico-cultural 'cause' to which he has remained devoted, even while the novelist in him has ensured the survival in his writer's imagination, as a precondition of authentic creative production, of enough of the distant and dispassionate 'balcony attitude to life' to ensure his fiction never became the mere mouthpiece of his personal convictions. There is to his novels a distinctive and at times mordant coolness of characterisation, observation and reflection, particularly when dealing with the issues closest to his heart. Referring to Graham Greene's famous remark that the novelist should always endeavour to keep a piece of ice in the heart, Humphreys has repeatedly emphasised that it is the sceptic in him that comes into play whenever he is engaged in writing fiction.

Hence his dispassionate, evenhanded analysis of such 'hot' subjects as the value of rural life, the treatment of which had driven so many Welsh writers of the interwar period either to overheated idealisation or to grotesquely deformed misrepresentations. During the course of his career, Humphreys has carefully balanced contrasting impressions of Welsh country living. The tendency of Jones, a middle-aged aesthete from the novel of the same name (1984), long fled to a pampered existence in London from the desperately poor small-holding of his early years, is to ignore the huge effort it had taken his labouring father to scrape a living. But that such labour can cripple the body and cramp the soul is evident in the case of Lucas in *Flesh and Blood* (1974), who has obstinately struggled to run the ironically named 'Swyn y Mynydd' ('Mountain Enchantment'), a tiny upland homestead on arid land thick with reeds, only to end up thoroughly embittered. Another novel, *A Change of Heart* (1951), unsparingly shows us Frank's disillusionment when his dreamy infatuation with a country girl gives way to a horror-stricken discovery of the brutal realities of farming life.

The careful dualities of Humphreys's treatment of Welsh rural life were prefigured in one of his very earliest poems. 'Unloading Hay' (*CP*, 4) heartily asserts that precisely because 'Heaven can be no soft and easy place', it must surely be 'Full of the country air, hard work and other country customs', but it is also careful to contain a reality check: 'This hay is not / So light and cloudy as perhaps it looks from the hill. / Its content is both rough and hard. Dead thistles / That preserve their bite, hard hay, hoar bits of hedges even.' Such writing is a conscious corrective to the seminal cult of the pious, cultured rural *gwerin* ('folk') as the backbone of the nation that had been promoted so assiduously in Welsh-language literature since the concluding years of the nineteenth century and that, albeit in modified form, was adopted as an important constituent even of the political programme of de-industrialisation and 'return to the land' that the Welsh National Party, Plaid Cymru, had been persuaded by Saunders Lewis to adopt during the Depression Thirties.[3] Indeed, Humphreys had himself been moved to work on the land during the Second World

War by a related belief that only by reconnecting with rural life could Wales survive the threats and changes attendant upon mass mobilisation and impending catastrophe.

Several of Humphreys's most important novels are in fact works of historical fiction in that they involve the excavation of key features of the states of mind of past periods. Hence his repeated fictional revisiting of the myth of the *gwerin*, as when an MP who greets Jones, in the novel of that name, on a train as a true son of the soil immediately comfortably employs the attendant clichés: 'I think the world of your father,' he sententiously intones, 'Salt of the earth. The very rock from which the best of our history is hewn.' (*J*, 9) Jones himself takes a different view of his origins, recalling the mucky farmyard and the stinking pigsty where his father used to imprison him when he was naughty. But sceptic that he is, even he instinctively reaches for another, positive, detail to balance his mental image: 'The oak tree and the pig sty. Title for a song perhaps. But certainly celebrate the tree. That one tree capable of outlasting and outliving a dynasty of pigsties.' (*J*, 2) An ancient archetypal image from the collective unconscious of the Welsh surfaces quietly and slyly in that image – the surface realism of Humphreys's novels frequently belies their underlying mythic significance. Jones is involuntarily recalling the seventh-century plight of Myrddin Wyllt, who became a mentally disturbed forest hermit after witnessing the bloody carnage of the Battle of Arfderydd (573 CE). His only refuge was a sturdy oak tree and his only companion a pig. Like many of Humphreys's characters, Jones the suave and sophisticated metropolitan may be anxious to be rid of his burdensome Welshness, but the ghostly paradigms of Welsh history continue to haunt him inexorably and he perforce plays out a role predetermined from his nation's past even while living his exiled life in a distant urban setting.

Like his fellow-countryman Raymond Williams, Humphreys is ever alive to the sharp social divisions within traditional rural society that give the lie to the pastoral myth of classlessness and the purported egalitarianism of *gwerin* life.[4] Central to both *The Little Kingdom* and *A Man's Estate* (1955) is the power within their own little realm wielded by the owners of substantial farms – the little garage owner Cornelius Evans, in the former novel, may ostensibly be the chapel equal of the large land-owner Richard Boyd, but there is never any doubt as to which of the two possesses true local weight. Boyd is the supreme autocrat of his own little realm, and there are many others like him in the fiction – Vavasor Elis in *A Man's Estate*, Kate's 'Pa' in *Outside the House of Baal*, 'Nain' of Glanrafon Stores in the *Land of the Living* sequence and so on. Such figures embody the hallowed values of a traditional rural community – respect for property, the security of land-ownership, the emphasis on tradition, the stability of custom – while also revealing the weaknesses of a social order closed to change and still retaining aspects of a 'feudal' world. Humphreys's critique of such a society is encapsulated in the view that in *A Man's Estate* Hannah, the inhibited spinster step-daughter of Vavasor Elis, sees framed in her window:

> I sit watching through my square window a man ploughing a field that slopes upwards. If I lean back this field fills all the window space except the top right which gives me a further horizon and a small view of the bay. The white gulls wheel perpetually around the tractor and the plough. Of course I cannot hear, but I know the narrow-faced young ploughman, Idwal, whistles as he leans back to admire his own work.
> The last time this field was ploughed I was twenty and Richard Davies grey then but fifteen years younger than he is now and free from rheumatism. (*ME*, 27)

That the scene she sees is so familiar, so comfortably knowable, is what makes it both attractive and dangerous. Humphreys here deliberately adopts the convention of representing rural life as timeless and as governed by the seasonal rhythms of nature only to subvert it by insinuating the stiflingly static, claustrophobic, character of such a lifelessly fixed existence.

He is, however, always respectful of the genuine claims to value of traditional Welsh country life. The elderly, tough-minded Kate in *Outside the House of Baal* may repeatedly recall her tyrannical father's miserly existence at Argoed, the extensive family farm, but she cannot condone her greedy brother Dan's action in selling the family's green acres to a property developer and remains attached in fond memory to the squabbling life she had once led in the company of her siblings in the family home. For timid little Iorwerth in *A Toy Epic*, his loving father's farm represents a permanent refuge: it is 'the headquarters of Noah', an ark firmly anchored against the raging floods of modernity – an image that recalls D. H. Lawrence's similarly lyrical evocations in the opening pages of *The Rainbow* of the farm life of the Brangwen family.[5] 'I followed my father to view the new hunt bull,' Iorwerth wistfully recalls, 'and my small fist groped along the resistant corduroy breeches he wore. The carthorse, the duck pond, the cowshed and the hay-shed, the stable and the granary constituted my city.' (*TE*, 17)

* * *

'I was brought up in a broad valley in one of the four corners of Wales', observes Michael at the opening of *A Toy Epic*, 'On fine days from my bedroom window I saw the sea curve under the mountains in the bottom right-hand corner of the window frame.' (*TE*, 7) Little Amy Parry in *Flesh and Blood* rejoices in a like glimpse from the hillside cottage of Swyn y Mynydd: 'From the top field there was a tantalising view of the sea.' (*FB*, 129) Tantalising indeed – so near yet so far. An entirely different world, in short, as in due course Amy, Michael and Iorwerth all realise when, during their progress towards adulthood, they undertake that short journey that is also a momentous *rite de passage* from their secluded inland homes to the brash coastal resorts. Appropriately enough, it is during the bus journey to her grammar school at Llanelw on the coast that Amy is suddenly excited to witness an aeroplane land-ing unexpectedly in a neighbouring field. And it is immediately after that that she meets Enid for the first time, the middle-class girl who is to become her closest friend and whose fate becomes inextricably intertwined with her own.

Although born in coastal Prestatyn, Humphreys himself was, of course, raised in the heart of the country but within sight of the sea.

27

And a formative experience in his own development was the discovery of the vast difference between the social character of his home village, Trelawnyd, and that of Rhyl, a bare seven miles distant, where he attended the County School. In his novels he conflated Rhyl and the neighbouring seaside town of Prestatyn to create a composite image of a north Wales coastal resort given over to catering for visitors and, increasingly, residents from the great English conurbation of the Liverpool-Manchester area. And to his imaginary town he gave the telling name 'Llanelw', a word which literally means 'Church of Profit.' Appropriately enough, it hints at a perversion of 'Llanelwy', the Welsh name for the little cathedral 'city' of St Asaph nearby. One is therefore the name of an ancient Welsh sacred site, the other the name given to a thoroughly anglicised town wholly given over to the worship of Mammon (or the biblical Baal, as Humphreys would alternatively term the pagan god of modern materialistic greed in what is indisputably his greatest novel).

For Amy's nationalist friend Enid, Llanelw is a shambles: cheap, nasty, and symbolic of a 'people . . . falling over themselves to sell their birthright for a mess of pottage.' Humphreys turns that very short journey of six miles from Trelawnyd to Rhyl, then, into a prefiguration of that engagement of a native with an aggressively invasive alien culture that is such a central theme of most of his fiction. And as is also so often true of that fiction, it is the Welsh middle class, all too eager to embrace the status and affluence of the English bourgeoisie, who bear the brunt of Enid's criticism. They are in places specifically associated with the old Welsh legend of the low-lying coastal region along Cardigan Bay – Cantre'r Gwaelod – that was forever lost to the rapaciously engulfing sea thanks entirely to the carelessness of a single watchman.

Partly perhaps because of his own origin as the son of a village headmaster, Humphreys's fiction is distinguished by its concentration on the ambivalent history of the modern Welsh middle class, the vulgar bulk of which is repeatedly shown to be in thrall to English values (his own parents had, after all, neglected to pass Welsh on to their son) leaving only an elite minority to remain stubborn guardians of the native language and its culture. And just as he had with Llanelw, he invented another coastal town – this time remotely situated on or near the Llŷn peninsula, and perhaps a conflation of Pwllheli and Porthmadoc – appropriately naming it 'Pendraw' ('The Terminal Point', in one of its senses). It, too, typified the many minor settlements across Wales run by a local class of shopkeepers, solicitors, school governors, local councillors and the like that remained fiercely loyal, throughout the early decades of the twentieth century, to the crown, the British Empire, and the Liberal Party under the fabled leadership of Lloyd George.

Typical of such a class is Councillor Hughes in *Flesh and Blood*, a self-important baker who dotes on his only daughter, Beti Buns, a gluttonous young woman, lean and ever craving some new sweet indulgence. Spoilt by her parents, the mincing Beti is prone to suffer a fit of asthma if she is crossed in any way. Faultlessly up to date with the latest fashions, she is a devotee of the Hollywood cinema of the 1930s and given to unintentionally comical renditions of the stars' favourite catchwords and theatrical poses. She is one of the many characters in the fiction that live a life of slavish mimicry of their supposed Anglo-American betters.

Humphreys is an accomplished satirist, with a sharp eye for social absurdities such as the formal attire of the Master of the Pendraw Workhouse. H. M. Meredith's pretensions in *Salt of the Earth* (1985) are all too visibly evident in his 'riding breeches with highly polished leggings' and in the glittering gold tiepin he carefully places 'behind the knot of his silk tie'. Such a panoply of weighty authority elicits sympathy from Tasker, an innocent observer, who gazes 'with compassion at the row of pens and pencils in Mr Meredith's waistcoat pockets. "You have great re-sponsibilities," Tasker said.' (*SE*, 98) The homes of such characters are likewise eloquently stuffed with social signifiers. When the young south Wales miner and communist agitator Pen Lewis finds himself in such a home, he is appropriately caustic:

> Pen moved his head and opened an eye wide to inspect the ornate sideboard against the wall. It was loaded with ornaments, photographs in silver frames and in the centre a bowl of wax fruit under a glass dome.

> 'What a place . . . Just look at it! The sideboard nudges the table and the table nudges the chair and the chair turns my legs into mahogany pit props.' (*SE*, 114–15)

This interior is designed to make the lower orders feel physically clumsy and thus socially inferior. In such an environment they seem to be metamorphosed into ungainly items of furniture themselves – after all, they are surrounded by the showily 'tasteful' appurtenances of a class that values things above people, or rather that judges people strictly according to the amount of property they have managed to acquire.

The later nineteenth century had seen the emergence across Wales for the first time, largely in the wake of the creation in the south east of a booming industrial economy, of a prosperous native Welsh middle class. Having found in the progressive wing of the Liberal Party of the day a powerful vehicle for the kind of religious, social and political reforms they demanded, most of the assiduously chapel-going members of the class became ardent supporters of that party. And their devotion was sealed by the spectacular ascent of David Lloyd George from Criccieth to key leadership roles in government during the first two decades of the twentieth century, culminating in his wartime service as Prime Minister. Those of Humphreys's novels that are concerned to examine the life of this era therefore concentrate of necessity on this Liberal ascendancy but only to critique it.

His was a deeply sceptical dissenting interpretation of the trajectory of Lloyd George's glittering political career. From his perspective it was the story of the complete betrayal of his early principles by a brilliant young Welsh nationalist who had all the gifts requisite for an authentic national hero, and his willing conversion into a lavishly rewarded and garlanded stooge of the English imperialist establishment. Lloyd George's great adversary, in Humphreys's account, was his polar opposite Saunders Lewis, who had remained true to his nationalist convictions and whose life and writings were a devastating indictment of the kind of social-climbing, London-orientated Welshness so typical for Humphreys of the Welsh people in general throughout their sorry history ever since the fateful Act of Union with England of 1536. Humphreys duly came to view Lewis as a combination of the two types of figures that have recurred throughout Welsh history and functioned as heroic guardians of Welsh identity: the prophet and the sacrificial victim.

Another of Lewis's polar opposites for Humphreys was Aneurin Bevan, the popular champion of a Welsh industrial proletariat and a glamorously left-wing figure in a determinedly centralist and unionist Labour Party that came to totally dominate the political life of Wales for a century following the Great War. An incomparable orator, rousing Socialist, self-proclaimed internationalist, generally credited with establishing the NHS within the Welfare Government of the post-war Attlee government, Bevan, in Humphreys's reading of his career, had followed Lloyd George's route to near the pinnacle of Westminster politics and had become similarly tamed by the English establishment. As for the gospel of Socialism preached by Bevan, Humphreys had some sympathy for its core aspirations as enshrined in the early Welfare State, but he soon became suspicious, rather like the George Orwell of *Animal Farm*, of its cult of the collective. And the strong centralist culture it developed seemed to him to replicate the animus against the respective national regions of the United Kingdom that had characterised a wartime Britain fixated on promoting a basically English and Imperialist patriotism embodied in the bellicose bulldog figure of Churchill.

Having grown to manhood during the 1930s, Humphreys had witnessed at first hand the malign collectivist experiments of Fascism and Stalin's Communism and become convinced that humankind needed, for its own good, to respect that insistence on the rights and related moral responsibilities of each and every individual, subject only to a strong concern for the general good, that had characterised nineteenth-century Welsh Nonconformity at its best. So strongly was he of this opinion during the 1950s that he took to styling himself a Protestant novelist – as distinct from his friend Graham Greene who was a self-confessed Catholic novelist, as were Evelyn Waugh and François Mauriac.[6] And he was never thereafter to abandon the tradition of conscientious dissent he saw as deriving from this commitment to a moral individualism. He accordingly came to see his own actions, essays and novels in defence of a threatened minority language as being part and parcel of this dissenting culture of steadfast, principled, public witness. It was this that impelled him to active support for the civil disobedience of the law-breaking campaigns on behalf of the language by Cymdeithas yr Iaith Gymraeg ('The Welsh Language Society') from the late 1960s through to the early 1980s.[7]

As for Bevan, while for many his stand against nuclear weapons seemed the very dissidence of principled dissent, Humphreys could see, in his name as well as his career, only a sad commentary on the modern Welsh condition. 'Nye' had after all been named after Aneirin, the seventh-century poet who was one of the great founding figures of the ancient and august Welsh-language literary tradition with which Bevan, who knew no Welsh, could feel absolutely no connection. For Humphreys he was, therefore, just another example – albeit like Lloyd George a stellar one – of the social-climbing Welsh who abound in his fiction. All are avid first for English recognition, then for English acceptance, and finally for English assimilation. As for Welsh Labour, its Unionist character was nowhere more apparent for Humphreys than in its cynical manipulation of the Investiture of the Prince of Wales at Caernarfon, 1969. A synthetic, made-for-television event, it was stage-managed by the malicious and oleaginous Secretary of State for Wales, George Thomas, to wrong-foot Plaid Cymru, the Welsh Nationalist Party, that had begun during the later 1960s to challenge Labour hegemony in Wales.[8]

* * *

But if Humphreys's views on the condition of Wales, as expressed in essays, interviews and *The Taliesin Tradition*, were trenchantly controversial, even incendiary, not so his treatment of related subjects in his novels, infused though they too basically are with his particular vision of Wales and the modern world. Far from being forthrightly polemic, the novels are elaborate, complex structures of ambivalence, ambiguity and indeterminacy. And his capacity to maintain an enabling distinction between his ideological commitments and his novelistic writing is nowhere more evident than in his fictional treatment of the social values and political culture of the motor region of industrial south Wales of which elsewhere he was so critical.

'The key to the future is the south-east . . . We've got to face that. The coalfield in particular.' (*BF*, 260) The words are those of Val Gwyn, a young, highly idealistic Welsh nationalist in *The Best of Friends* (1978), whose own background in the cultivated Welsh-speaking society of a predominantly rural north Wales means that for him, as for Humphreys himself, 'the valleys' of south-east Wales are virtually a foreign country whose values and customs he has to struggle to understand. But that life throughout the whole of Wales is becoming increasingly influenced, and indeed profoundly reshaped, by this powerful 'alien' industrial culture becomes evident to Val when he happens upon the corpse of a miner, recently choked to death by the coal-dust in his lungs, hidden in the hay of a barn deep in the Welsh countryside.

The historical setting for this scene is, of course, that of the dread Depression years of the 1930s, when the industrial valleys experienced social devastation. It was the perfect breeding ground for radical politics, and Val, when he ventures South, soon finds himself face-to-face with Pen Lewis, a young miner and brilliant Communist organiser, whose electric virility and animal vitality contrast with the pallid, etiolated body and intellectual fastidiousness of Val. Pen it is who laughingly dismisses the relevance of Val's particular version of Welshness to the experiences of his own world: 'What's the Welsh for "victimisation?" he said. 'What's the Welsh for "dialectical materialism?" What's the Welsh for "bicycle," for God's sake?' (*BF*, 281) And Val's response? It is to point out lamely that his antagonist's full name is 'Penry Aneurin Lewis', a name that betrays the latent existence in his core identity of that very Welsh-language culture whose irrelevance to his own case he seeks mockingly to demonstrate.

33

Amy Parry, the young heroine not only of *The Best of Friends* but of the septet of novels in the *Land of the Living* series of which it is but a part, is torn between the respective claims and attractions of the gentle Val, for whom she feels an instinctive moral admiration and intellectual respect, and Pen, to whose physical magnetism, sexual vigour and mercurial wit she helplessly succumbs. And needless to say, Amy's plight mirrors Humphreys's analysis of that aspect of the Welsh predicament during the Depression 1930s that most fascinates him: a country caught between the competing claims of the Red Dragon and the Red Flag, Welsh nationalism and the Socialist International. And if the sexual inhibitions and virtual impotence of Val mirror the author's concerns about the ability of the world he represents to create a flourishingly modern society, then the blithe intellectual self-denial of the casually promiscuous Pen suggests a society cheerfully hell-bent on abandoning all the traditional markers that have sustained a distinctively different Welsh identity.[9]

One thing is certain: Pen is a creature of the Valleys through and through, while Val can never be anything but an outsider there. Even his attempts to negotiate the industrial terrain are physically ludicrous, so that 'Pen laughed out loud when he saw Val leap into the air to clear a derelict hen-coop first and then skip up again to avoid a broken bedstead sticking out of a hole in the ground. "A bloody kangaroo," Pen said. "That's all he is. An overgrown schoolboy."' (*BF*, 273) But if Pen the Welsh Communist seems to revel and thrive amidst the detritus of industrialism, believing that in it lies the seeds of a revolutionary future, Val and Amy can see there nothing but a wasteland. For them that depressing scene of social dereliction signifies the dead-end of a way of life, founded on the positive aspects of late nineteenth-century religious Nonconformity that for all its glaring faults had once been instinct with the possibility of a vibrantly distinctive Welsh future.

The watershed event for Humphreys was the First World War, roughly coinciding with the end of the bourgeois Cymru Fydd ('Young Wales') era that had seen the establishing of so many key national institutions such as the University of Wales and the

National Museum. The Great War ensured the collapse of the Non-conformist religious and social order that had underpinned Cymru Fydd, leaving a lost, culturally disorientated generation. In 1988, Humphreys emphasised 'the explosive nature of the impact of the Great War on the sedate and almost somnolent order of our grand-parents. It was as if a bomb had been thrown into the middle of a Sunday School treat'. (*CR*, 82) It also resulted in an industrial crisis that precipitated the transfer of political control from Liberal to Labour, and created a new, class-based proletarian identity. It is therefore appropriate that Amy Parry, young, beautiful, intel-lectually gifted and determinedly ambitious, should be an orphan born at the turn of the century, and raised on a scrape-acre small-holding by devout, morally stern step-parents whose beliefs and values she quickly abandons. It is through charting Amy's progress over seven linked novels from penurious childhood before the First World War through a rebelliously nationalistic young adult-hood to an old age comfortably bedecked with jewels and garlanded with the highest English honours, that Humphreys is able deftly to track the profound social changes, bewildering political shifts and complex ideological conflicts of twentieth-century Welsh history. Amy's prominent social 'success' and acceptance into the heart of the English establishment represents Humphreys's fear that Wales, too, is destined in the not-too-distant future to be comfortably assimilated into England.

* * *

The creative effort made, then, by Humphreys, in several of his best novels, to capture the climate of thinking as much as the social, economic and political realities of the period from the Great War down to the Second World War, underlines the fact that he is, by deepest inclination, a historical novelist. And he has made related efforts to capture key features of the *mentalité* of the later decades of the twentieth century as well. Thus, *Hear and Forgive* examines the optimism associated with the heady early years of the Welfare State, along with the intoxicating release of individual energies that was the legacy of the wartime erosion of social distinctions and softening of class divisions. The attractive but equivocal idealism of 1960s America is captured in *The Anchor Tree* (1980), while the cynical opportunism that heralded the arrival of Thatcherian politics is dryly anatomised in *Jones*.

As for *The Gift*, one of several novels by Humphreys to have been consistently overlooked and underrated, it engages critically with the ethos of the Britain of the Macmillan years, with their telling slogans of 'You've never had it so good,' and 'I'm all right, Jack.' A definitive feature of this period, for Humphreys, was the rival claims of a Socialist Welfare State, with its privileging of the needs and claims of the masses, on the one hand, and those of the rampant, ruthlessly competitive economic individualism of a new boom phase of capitalism on the other. Typical products of the latter environment in the fiction include such odious characters as the duplicitous Welshman Jenkins, ever ready to smile his most friendly smile: 'Hadn't I heard him say, where was it? When? . . . in exactly that nasal fruity voice that issued so confidently always from that big, dangling head, *"If you are going to cut somebody's throat you may as well do it with a smile."'* (*G*, 294)

In such a polarised world, Humphreys's sympathies lie with a character such as Uncle Alfred, an unkempt old man enfeebled by age, who is carted off to prison in an ambulance for non-payment of taxes as a protest against state deployment of weapons of mass destruction. '"It's at moments like this,"' says Alfred to his young friend Halkin, '"that a man becomes aware of the social force of gravity. He becomes aware that he is being swallowed by the great mass of Inertia and consent we call the Will of the People."' (*G*, 273) It is a realisation that also dawns on his young niece Polly, when she too climbs into the ambulance to keep him company. They have both, she feels, been '"swallowed up, deprived of their independence . . . at the mercy of the machinery of society"'. (*G*, 277) The scene typifies Humphreys's concern that the post-war period would be characterised not by the openly sinister totalitarianism of the pre-war ideological systems he had known but rather by controlling ideologies of a subtle, insidiously hidden, and therefore much more dangerous kind. Having lived as a young man in the dark shadow of the monstrous systems of the 1930s and having grown up in what he regarded as a colonised Welsh environment, Humphreys has always been exceptionally sensitive to the symptoms of what Gramsci would have called hegemonic control. And he has accordingly been alive to the covert ideological aspects of the immensely powerful modern mass media industries of film and of broadcasting of which he has had considerable personal experience.

In *The Italian Wife* Richard Miller is a film magnate, as well as prospective Labour candidate, newspaper proprietor, and unprincipled opportunist. He is also an embodiment of the lucrative marriage of convenience during the 1960s between an ostensibly altruistic socialist establishment and the buccaneering enterprise of an unfettered economic individualism. But the advent of the Welfare State could precipitate genuine moral dilemmas as well as nurture moral corruption. Edward Allenside, in *Hear and Forgive*, is the headmaster of a London comprehensive school, newly established after the war to ensure parity of opportunity for students of all social backgrounds. But while the deep sincerity of his own good intentions as educationalist are beyond question, he becomes increasingly concerned that he may have unintentionally betrayed his own socialist principles by capitulating to the wishes of the dictatorial senior governor of the school. On anguished reflection, Allenside comes to fear he may have done so only in order to advance his own career interests and so compromised his moral integrity. His rueful conclusions are that '"For three years I have been able to deceive myself. It's frightening to know we find bigger ways of making fools of ourselves as we get older. We shake off the wilder illusions in order to adopt the subtler kind that aren't so obviously ridiculous."' (*HF*, 109)

Concern with such issues was, of course, typical of Humphreys throughout the 1950s, when he was first developing and then elaborating his concept of the duties of a Protestant novelist for whom obedience to the dictates of individual moral conscience must always be paramount. But at the same time he recognised that endless self-examination of this kind could become not only neurotically disabling but even, paradoxically, morally unbalanced and destructive of human relations. It is with the torment of such a sick moral conscience that David Flint struggles in *Hear and Forgive*, having left his wife to live with the socially advantageous niece of a powerful school governor. As for Humphreys himself, his fiction has continued throughout his career to foreground examples of fateful moral choice, long after he had ceased explicitly to identify as a Protestant novelist. And along with such other characteristics of his imagination as a rooted recognition of innate human sinfulness (the secular residue of the Calvinist theology of original sin), a quizzical interest in deterministic philosophies of various kinds (the secular shades of Calvinist predestination), and a penchant for judgments variously subtle, complex, equivocal and trenchant, they are a permanent confirmation that he is indeed the distinguished heir of the Welsh Nonconformist tradition of which he remains a professed, though far from uncritical, admirer. 'To understand a nineteenth-century Welshman, and indeed for a twentieth-century Welshman to understand himself,' he has written, 'it is essential to know to which denomination or religious sect his immediate ancestors belonged.' (*TT*, 101)

3

PROTESTANT NOVELIST

Given that issues of moral choice have remained central to Humphreys the novelist throughout his career,[1] it is interesting to note that when first he made his appearance in print in 1939, in Keidrych Rhys's madcap pioneering journal of Anglo-Welsh literature and culture *Wales*, it was in the company of such writers as Dylan Thomas, Lynette Roberts, Vernon Watkins and R. Williams Parry,[2] and with a poem sententiously entitled '1536–1936: A Young Man Considers His Prospects.' (*CP*, 1) 1536 was of course the date of the Act of Union of Wales with England; 1936 the date of Penyberth and Humphreys's personal awakening. At the outset of his career, Humphreys very much believed that his future as an author was likely to lie in poetry – indeed, his very first attempt at a novel had been written in verse. And, with an awareness made precociously mature by the threat of impending war and the uncertainty of his surviving it, he outlined with a grave wit in this early poem the three options by which as a young Anglo-Welsh writer of his time he seemed to be faced.

The first was to be an assiduous cultivator of the English literary establishment, carefully content to 'accept the current creeds, / Never be awkward in my beliefs, a path that leads / To fines, imprisonment or social outlawry'. That way he stood a reasonable chance of ending up dying 'an honourable old man'. The second was to be a fastidiously uncommitted aesthete, dedicated to nothing but serving his 'art', in the manner of Humphreys's bête noir at that time, James Joyce. The third option was to play 'Boswell to the dying Wales', which would inevitably mean having to 'Remark careers and graph the tongue's decay, / Industries dying; people going away; / And standing on a rock above the tide / Watch hostile waters rise on every side.' (*CP*, 1) What Humphreys of course omitted to mention was the fourth option – which no doubt he was yet to discover – namely of committing himself not to merely faithfully observing and recording the death of a people and their language but to intervening actively, as author as well as activist, in an attempt to arrest and if possible reverse the processes that were threatening to lead to such an apocalyptic conclusion.

Humphreys consciously chose, then, to confront himself with a profound and fateful moral choice at the very moment when he was setting out to make himself an author. His novels accordingly afford a whole repertoire of moments and occasions of ethical choosing, several of which bring out the dry, caustic wit to which he is often moved when dealing with the history of a dominated and marginalised little people such as the servile and demurely compliant Welsh, long used to practising deception and self-decep- tion in an attempt to curry favour with the English establishment and thus secure advancement. But that wit can take on a somewhat melancholy, even tragic, complexion at times too, as when the naively idealistic young nationalist Val Gwyn is easily enticed in *The Best of Friends* into a morally compromising alliance with the wily old hand and anglicised Establishment grandee Sir William Prosser. '"I may be a foolish and impulsive old fogey,"' Sir William confesses to a fascinated Val with a winning if disingenuous honesty,

"but I want to do something good for this little country of ours before I cross that frontier from which no traveller returns. I want to pay my debt to the ancestors that made me what I am and gave me what I now honestly believe to be the better part of me. I want to ensure that their values and their vision shall not perish from the earth." (*BF*, 195)

The scene predictably ends with Sir William magnanimously extending his hand to the mesmerised Val, who takes it eagerly and trustingly. It is a sinister gesture that is repeated in much of Humphreys's work, as when in his very first published novel, *The Little Kingdom*, the nauseatingly self-satisfied Welsh MP Carrog

Ellis places a fatherly hand on the knee of Owen Richards, the young Welsh Nationalist with whom he happens to be sharing a carriage on their separate journeys to London.

As for the central action of *The Little Kingdom*, it raises the issue of moral choice to the same tragic level that it occupies in Dostoevsky's great novel *Crime and Punishment*, a work of which at times it seems a distant echo: it features a murder committed in the name of a general good so great that it is judged by the protagonist Owen Richards to justify the most morally repugnant of individual actions. Owen sincerely convinces himself that killing his uncle will enable him to save a tract of land destined to be sold to the government for the building of a military aerodrome that would destroy the culture of the local community.

It is instantly evident, then, that this plot is both an uncanny reflection and a sinister distortion of the Penyberth incident, where the activists involved had been very clear to distinguish between a symbolic strike against what they saw as property specifically intended to prepare the British State for armed conflict and any harm to humans, to which they were totally opposed. And in deliberately distorting their actions Humphreys was not intending either to undermine their aims and accomplishments or to repudiate his own firm support of them, but rather to reflect on the inescapably ambivalent character of the tenets and assumptions underlying the whole episode. Consequently, his treatment of Penyberth in this, the very first of his novels to be published, was a prefiguration of what was to be his practice throughout his subsequent long writing career. Far from being the mouthpieces for his own ideology, his novels were always to serve as experimental laboratories, in which many of the values closest to his heart were subjected to repeated intense cross-examinations that invariably produced deeply equivocal results.

At the opposite pole from the case of Owen Richards is that of Jones, the confirmed Welsh exile in the novel of that name, the ostensible prominent 'success' of whose London life has been determined by his early decision to ignore whatever moral claims his native country of Wales may have had upon him. But now, in his declining years and an increasingly decrepit figure no longer to be satisfied by his substantial wealth, his fickle friends or his many casual lovers, Jones the pathetic, narcissistic loner is left to contemplate daily routines empty of purpose: 'Don't go back to bed. Shave. Make a cup of tea. Light a cigarette. Enjoy your wealth. Sink into it like a sensuous experience. Shuffle about all day in bedroom slippers. There's nothing calling.' (J, 137)

For Humphreys, the construction of plots is inseparable from the tracking of moral choices, because as he once wrote, it is plot that 'presents the independently living characters of a novel with situations in which they are forced to act, to make a choice, to consider right and wrong, human destiny, their own destiny and salvation'. (CR, 71) It is a conception of plot that is as old as Aristotle himself, since it was he who famously insisted that it was always actions that revealed the deep biases of character, hence the centrality of the analysis of plot in his famous thesis on 'stage' tragedy, The Poetics. Humphreys has accordingly always considered himself to be in essence a 'classical' novelist, as distinct from the Modernists, many of whom were in his view content with, even intent upon, the abandonment of traditional plotting. One of Humphreys's novels, The Italian Wife, had actually been consciously modelled on Phaedra by Euripides, partly no doubt because he was concerned to bestow the dignity of authentic tragic stature on his central characters.

Humphreys's 'Nonconformist' insistence on the primacy of personal moral responsibility, bolstered by an interest in Kierkegaardian existentialism, has meant that, while admittedly benefiting from Freudian insights into the motors of human action hidden deeply in the unconscious, he has also resisted the deterministic conclusions towards which unqualified acceptance of Freud's work might be said to tend. A case in point is that of young Gwen, in The Change of Heart, who confesses to her lover Frank that she is of illegitimate birth, adding that it is guilt on this score that involuntarily prompts her to act so selfishly and irresponsibly. But as the action of the novel gradually makes clear, this is in reality no more than a convenient rationalisation; an excuse for looking to whomever happens to be at hand for succour, comfort and satisfaction. Similarly, once Amy Parry, the heroine of the epic *Land of the Living* sequence, has persuaded herself that she was very hard done by when young, she feels licensed to 'compensate' for this by dedicating her whole life to the pursuit of conspicuous wealth and social prestige, whatever the cost to friends, family, lovers or country. And likewise Roger Allenside in *Hear and Forgive* is ever ready to justify his own unprincipled, deceitful, manipulative behaviour as an understandable and forgivable reaction against his hated and supposedly hateful step-father.

But always counterbalancing Humphreys's emphasis on individual conscience is his awareness that an individual life is inextricably interwoven with the collective(s) of which he or she is an inescapable part. Interactions and relationships are therefore intimately constitutive of any and every individual being, as Humphreys's great hero Saunders Lewis had repeatedly emphasised:

> Man is a social being. It is within society alone that the dignity of his existence lies. It is through society alone that he can find personal fulfilment. Everything that an individual ever accomplished, the achievements of intellect and imagination as expressed in image and picture and architecture, was accomplished only through cooperation and collective endeavour. He must socialise. He must love and cherish his social environment. Is it not therefore inevitable that anyone who rebels against his society and rejects it is in fact denying himself a full and fulfilling life, is imperceptibly destroying himself, is emasculating himself?[3]

Old-fashioned and embarrassingly gendered in their phrasing though such sentiments are nowadays likely to seem, they remain of value because they illuminate the kind of thinking that is inscribed in Humphreys's novels. And in some of them, he uses heavily stylised monologue to convey the dangerously inward turn of the characters' minds and lives. Hannah, in *A Man's Estate*, for instance, fantasises about a saviour who will miraculously deliver her from her spinsterish 'captivity'. Such utopian dreams are a symptom of her arrested development and are the negative expression of her stultifying social rootedness. As for her brother Philip, who has experienced a separate and different upbringing, he is impaired in a contrary way. Removed from his mother at an early age, and lacking roots in either place or family, he has become selfish, egotistic, self-sufficient and incapable of real human reciprocity. Owen Richards suffers from a like condition in *The Little Kingdom*, except that in his case excessive solitariness has resulted in a belief in his own superior existence. Conceiving of himself as a kind of Übermensch or Superman, he ventures to defy the moral law, repudiating it as nothing but a social convention.

> She doesn't understand, Owen was thinking. She doesn't realise that I am more than just an ordinary man of goodwill eager to serve my country. This inward knowledge and certainty of power that I have is not yet to be shared with others. It is a burden to be borne alone. In the end I am always alone. Loneliness is the penalty of the explorer and the prophet. No amount of furs can keep out its cold wind. It needs more than physical endurance. (*LK*, 156)

When he was writing this novel as the war was drawing to its conclusion, the evil narcissism of Hitler and of Mussolini were still naturally very present in Humphreys's mind.

It was his interest in the creation of a form adequate for tracing the intricacies of human interrelationships within the confines of a given society that led Humphreys to devise fictions based on a sequence of short scenes, various interlinked and contrasting, that allowed him to present characters and actions in a rapid succession of differing perspectives. The purpose, as indeed the result, of this kaleidoscopic approach was to prevent any rash rush to judgement on the part of a reader, and to promote an interpretative process the outcome of which was bound to be complex and nuanced. 'At the heart of each significant situation,' he once commented, 'there is a mystery.' (*CR*, 75) He had in mind the inalienable mystery of human character, which as a novelist he has always been very anxious to recognise and respect. For Tolstoy and Dostoevsky, he added, 'life was more than the raw material of art; it was a strange sea in which humanity thrashed about like a powerful, bewildered whale, harpooned by death, and still consumed with a desire for Immortality.' (CR, 71)

Consider, for example, his novel *A Change of Heart*. The title would seem to lead us to expect that it is preoccupied with a good old-fashioned theme. At the beginning, Frank is very willing to blame Howell, the husband, for the infidelity of his wife Lucy, who is Frank's sister. But by the end of the novel, he has seen the light, recognising that it is Lucy, rather, who has been taking unscrupulous advantage of her soft-hearted and all-too-complaisant husband. Or so it would seem on the surface – until, that is, one begins to factor in the fact that during the course of the novel Frank has become bitterly disillusioned with his two-timing lover, Gwen, who he believes has betrayed him. Is it therefore not possible that the 'change of heart' manifest in his condemnation of Lucy is nothing but a projection on to her, now seen as a scheming, cheating female, of his feelings of resentment towards Gwen? And *Hear and Forgive* has a similar twist in its tail. Throughout the novel, the novelist David Flint is tortured by the knowledge that he has left his wife for his sophisticated mistress Helen primarily in order to advance his own career. And by the novel's end he has returned to his family. But the primary reason for that development is not any decision reached by David, but rather the fact that Helen has chosen to abandon him. And as for his reconciliation with his family, how sincere and lasting can that possibly be, given that he continues to despise them at heart?

It is indeed very difficult for any human being to know from what direction authentic 'salvation' may come. As can be seen from *The Italian Wife*, the act of 'choosing' can be a dauntingly complex one in the human context. Paola is a sensitive, conscientious and sympathetic woman married to a wastrel. It is then her misfortune to fall in love with her step-son, Chris. Despite her very best efforts to master her passion, she yields in the end to the advice of her worldly friend, Cecilia, that she confide to Chris her feelings towards him. From there on things assume an ever worsening complexion. It is no wonder, therefore, that Humphreys should have shrewdly observed in one of his essays that in real life pre-destination and freedom of will (and therefore of choice) are by no means the polar opposites they are in logic.

His interest in such matters inevitably means that Humphreys has always regarded himself as belonging in the company of the great European novelists of manners and morals, and that he has always demonstrated a keen interest in those singular identifying features that characterise particular societies at particular periods. One example of such is his interest in the prominent part played by machines in twentieth-century Western society. The fact that Dic, Albie's father in *A Toy Epic*, is a bus driver endows him with particular glamour in the eyes of his proud young son and his friends Michael and Iorwerth. For them, living as they do in their secluded inland valley, the bus represents an exciting link with the wider world of experience they so yearn to enter. Little do they know that poor Dic is plagued by the indigestion that comes from doing nothing all day but sitting passively behind a wheel, or that he complains daily of being shaken to death by the rattling old vehicle he is condemned to drive. Only as they grow up are the boys capable of taking a more balanced view of the Big Red Bus that had so seduced their childish imaginations as to seem an ambassador sent from distant, exotic parts. The capacity of a machine, in the modern age, to function as a status symbol is con-veyed in *The Little Kingdom* by the way that Boyd, the wealthy farmer, drives his car: 'To Boyd's eyes, focused along the black bonnet of the limousine, the view was too familiar to notice, like a railway-station poster.' (*LK*, 14) He is insulated from his world in much the same way that his nephew Owen Richards's megalo-mania insulates him from the moral implications of his action in murdering his uncle, and this, too, is suggested by the inordinately long and narrow bonnet of the car he has opted to drive. It is an apt symbol for the raptor in him, for his lust for dominating every-one and everything. As for Tom Siôn Bodlon, a poor unfortunate doomed to become Richards's prey, he has no idea how an engine works, proud owner though he may be of a motorbike.

In *The Best of Friends*, the nerdish young poet and intellectual John Cilydd looks like Don Quixote on his Rosinante when mounted on the back of his motorbike, his leather gear turning him into a latter-day gallant knight in armour. Needless to say he is too much the dreamer ever to be fully in control of his machine. The habit of Sali Prytherch of gaily abandoning her little car at odd angles when parking is powerfully expressive of the social confidence that came in the 1930s with being one of His Majesty's Inspector of Schools. Her car is, of course, a racy 'roadster', reflecting the jauntiness of the first generation of young women to be granted a measure of social freedom and licence in the immediate aftermath of the First World War. By the time the 1970s arrived the fashion had changed in cars as in everything else, and so Jones's car of choice, as he scuttles around London on his own self-absorbed business, is a VW Beetle. Since Richard Miller, in *The Italian Wife*, relies wholly on the car to carry him to his illicit affairs, it is inevitable that his woes should begin in earnest only when the car breaks down.

Examples of Humphreys's use of cars as significant social signifiers could, then, be multiplied indefinitely. A particularly egregious example occurs in *The Anchor Tree*, Humphreys's 'American' novel, central to which is his depiction of the car-dump of the pathetically thuggish Heber S. Hayes, a lump of paranoid aggression intent on nothing but defending his own property against all comers and at all costs in the classic tradition of American individualism in its most brutish form. Within the novel, such a car dump functions in much the way that the rubbish dump so famously does in Scott Fitzerald's *The Great Gatsby*, as a symbol of the appalling moral squalor that lies at the very heart of American affluence: 'Auto wrecks had been dragged straight off the road and were piled up as far as they would go into the trees.' (*AT*, 63) It is not surprising, therefore, to discover that the dump is effectively reducing a whole forest to a state of devastation similar to its own: 'a form of warfare had already broken out, threatening fire and destruction and the black decay of a burnt deserted woodland.' (*AT*, 63) The image fuses anxieties about acquisitive Western society's appallingly destructive and wasteful practices with the fear of nuclear disaster that haunted the 1960s mind of the West in general but of the USA in particular. Wandering among the debris, young Grover happens upon an arresting sight:

> He shaded his eyes to point out a powerful pine that served as the mast of a block and tackle system that hoisted wrecks in the air in order to stack them roughly on top of each other.
>
> There's the anchor tree, he said. Hub of the universe. A jib projected from it. A wreck hung up in the air, both doors hanging open like a scarecrow on a gibbet. (*AT*, 65)

This passage offers us a powerful example of Humphreys's ability to create an organising symbol – a symbol, that is, the implications of which reach out resonantly throughout the text to draw widely scattered events into a single, deeply revealing order. Such devices serve to integrate a novel and to focus, concentrate and amplify its meanings. One of the most famous Modernist examples of this practice is the deployment by Virginia Woolf of the island lighthouse as organising symbol in the aptly entitled *To the Lighthouse* (1927). In like manner, Humphreys refers in the title *Outside the House of Baal* to the organising symbol of the pub, that appears in the novel to be the seat of the modern hedonistic materialism that threatens to destroy all the old collective values traditionally centred, in the case of Wales, on the chapels. The reference is to the crucial episode in the Old Testament when Elijah, trusting to his Judaic faith in the Almighty, defeats the priests of the cruel pagan god Baal. Whether this miraculous feat can be repeated in the twentieth century is, as the novel makes very clear, extremely unlikely.

Therefore, on the outcome of the 'choice' facing the Welsh people – if 'choice' is the appropriate term for the nebulous, mysterious and labyrinthine process by which a society at large steers its course in one direction rather than another – hangs the very survival of Wales as a nation. The options are either to conform happily and comfortably to the ways of a modern consumer society increasingly global and culture-blind in character, or to attempt resolutely to reconnect not so much with the 'chapel world', which Humphreys well knows has disappeared forever, but with the rich body of values, principles and practices fostered by that world at its best – riddled with hypocrisies and a legion of other faults though the Welsh Nonconformist establishment may well have been at its repugnant worst. What is perhaps worth emphasising at this point is that whereas Humphreys's position on this 'choice' has always been clear *outside* of his fiction, his treatment of it in *Outside the House of Baal* itself is memorable and compelling precisely because the 'conclusions' reached within the confines of the text are so problematic, debatable and indeed essentially indeterminate.

* * *

And so we come back again to that little word 'choice' that seems to loom large over every one of Humphreys's texts. For him, it is the peculiar fate of every Welsh individual to have to face up to this challenge to choose, precisely because the survival of a stateless Wales itself has always been, as it will always remain for the foreseeable future, dependent on a perpetual act of choice and an exercise of the will by its people – what the Breton historian Renan famously called 'a daily plebiscite'.[4] It follows that for Humphreys the very same duty is incumbent on every Welsh writer and artist worth her or his salt, despite the huge temptation to forgo it that is so feelingfully voiced by Geraint in *The Little Kingdom*:

> *Oh, I wish I hadn't to make a decision over this.* It weighed on his mind unbearably. As though he hadn't enough to make him miserable already. *Why can't I be left alone?* His contribution to the national life was in literature. How worthily he could contribute if only he were given the chance. Several critics had said he was a promising young writer. (*LK*, 184)

Humphreys attributed this artistic attachment to the cult of the unfettered individual to English Romanticism, seeing it augmented in the stance of many of the most prominent Modernists and balefully instanced in Wales in the career of Dylan Thomas.

His preferred model by contrast was the Saunders Lewis who had refused to distinguish between 'aesthetic and moral choice', and whose greatness was to be attributed directly to the intimate connection between the products of his artistic imagination and the history of his nation.

Humphreys was acutely aware, however, that in his own case the making of such vivifying connections was complicated, and could indeed even be fatefully inhibited, by his need to write in English, fluent Welsh speaker though he had become. In this respect, too, he came to view himself as a border writer – inhabiting the desolate no-man's land between one language and culture and another, endlessly attempting to mediate the one to the other, saddled with the thankless task of performing the unappreciated role of an honest broker. He therefore knew the temptation to take the easy way out – to use the Welsh-language background to which he had gained privileged admittance merely as the raw material for colourful writing in English, cunningly calculated to satisfy the vulgar expectations of readers the far side of Offa's Dyke. His novels include several examples of such lucrative abdications of responsibility as we see in the case of Eddie Meredith, one of life's beguiling chameleons and natural 'performers', who attempts to persuade the young Welsh-language activist and writer John Cilydd Moore to follow his own example in *Salt of the Earth*:

> Do you know what? I had the most marvellous idea last night for a murder mystery. People love murder mysteries. Set in Pendraw of course. A preacher comes by with a portable pulpit. Children began to disappear. The townsfolk blame everyone. And all the time it's the preacher that's guilty. (*SE*, 148)

Humphreys is here satirising those numerous Anglo-Welsh writers – Dylan Thomas and Caradoc Evans prominent amongst them – who had thrived outside Wales by turning Welsh Nonconformity into the butt of their grotesque comedies. And Humphreys also had in mind the kind of strangulated English such writers had invented in order to pander to the ignorant perception that Welsh was nothing but a primitive patois. His own response was to write his novels in a plain English adequate not only for dealing with English-speaking characters but also for conveying the impression that for Welsh-speakers their own language was a perfectly normal instrument of thought and expression. To misapply Barthes's term, Humphreys chose to 'write white',[5] that is to write normatively, in a standard English bleached of the 'colour of saying' for which the Anglo-Welsh writing of the previous generation had become notorious.

That Eddie's milieu is that of film is no surprise since the creatures from that world are frequently depicted by Humphreys in a highly unfavourable light. That is because he is prone to view them as the sorcerers of modern society, endowed with a highly ambivalent power to mesmerise the masses and entice them to follow these Pied Pipers of the modern world of mass visual media. But such an estimation of actors is balanced by his great admiration for what their profession is capable of accomplishing at its responsible best, and for the moral as well as the aesthetic courage displayed by a profession that risks a failure every day that will be every bit as public as success. Having worked so closely with actors, Humphreys retained a profound and fascinated appreciation of the equivocal character of their calling.

In Eddie Meredith, acting talent takes on an impish, even devilish, character as his capacity to act the tempter is greatly enhanced by the sexual attractiveness that can also often be one of the most valuable assets of performers. Meredith sets out to seduce John Cilydd, sensing the currents of homosexual desire coursing through his veins secretly, since he has internalised his Welsh Puritan society's proscription of any such practice. Cilydd is the tortured victim of his society's intolerance, and he finds it excruciatingly difficult to break free from its toils, even though he is sensitive and intelligent enough to understand that a failure to do so is likely to break him as an individual and to prevent the development of his major poetic talent. Cilydd's plight therefore introduces us to the dark side of Welsh-language culture at its most appallingly conservative.

An examination of this particular case is a salutary corrective to any supposition that Humphreys takes a naively untroubled and wholly approving view of the relation between the Welsh artist and his society. Which is hardly surprising, given the history of his hero, Saunders Lewis, who had made himself a social outcast from the very society he was committed to defending, first by converting to Catholicism and then by setting fire to Penyberth. One of the great Welsh-language poets of the day, R. Williams Parry, accordingly likened Lewis to a great exotic bird that had suddenly alighted in a farmyard full of poultry: 'You stooped from your heaven to the grains on the cosy yard / Blinding with your colour all the chicks and pullets; / And created in the dove-cote doors above your head / The old, old flutter that occurs among doves.'[6] Lewis 'the forsaken one, a fool' had, as he himself later put it, consciously decided to offer himself as redemptive victim on the altar of his nation's memory. While the religiose phrasing may cause us today to flinch, it is still possible to admire the actions that flowed from his sacrifice. And Lewis's case, paralleling as it does in some ways that of John Cilydd, is a reminder that Humphreys was, from the very beginning, fully aware that the irrevocable commitment he had deliberately chosen to make to dedicate his life and his art to the service of his country was fraught with risk both for himself personally and for his talent.

Moreover, Humphreys was also aware that however dedicated an artist might be to challenging the values of established society, he or she was always very likely to depend on that society for a living, and so was bound to some extent to reach some kind of working compromise with it. Hence, no doubt, the interest he shows in his fiction in the relationship between an aspiring individual and the 'patron' who supports her or his work psychologically, practically or financially. Such are the relationships between Chris and his friend Bert in *The Italian Wife*, Frank and Howell in *A Change of Heart*, and David Flint and his lover in *Hear and Forgive*.

This last is a particularly interesting example since, although it is one of the group of early novels not to be either set in or concerned with Wales, it is the only instance of Humphreys dealing explicitly in his fiction with the experience of being a novelist. Moreover, the treatment of this subject is such as to suggest that he is transposing to an English context the dilemmas that for him specifically confront a Welsh writer of fiction. David Flint is a writer who comes from a poor underprivileged region of England, which is why he has been magnetically attracted to the great metropolis of London. He hungers for the success that alone can compensate for his lowly early background. As for the hedonistic lifestyle he accordingly adopts, for Humphreys it signifies the very attitude towards the arts that he himself deplores in his essay on the theatre of Saunders Lewis. There he writes of how hedonism can stand for 'a perspective on life that grants the artist free creative licence to develop his/her own potential whatever the obstacles in the way', and at whatever cost to others or to society at large. To which he adds: 'and isn't that the very kind of lonely hedonism that we find instanced in the colourful career of Dylan Thomas?'[7] Humphreys has always been particularly severe on any artist who seems to have abdicated social responsibility, just as his own artistic philosophy has involved a core belief in the need for a critically vigilant social commitment.

The psychology of the creative artist also receives some attention in *Hear and Forgive*. 'It was a secretive process,' David Flint reflects, 'like keeping an intimate diary that one day everyone could read. Not a noble profession at all; but like watching a spider, an obsession half way between a hobby and a science.' (*HF*, 17) It is no doubt a view of the matter that occurs naturally to Humphreys as he is consciously the heir of a Puritan tradition in which the daily duty of rigorous spiritual self-examination has always loomed large. While his comments elsewhere on the subject amount to no more than a casual scattering of remarks in various essays and interviews, they do include rueful reflections on the ruthlessly selfish and predatory nature of writers, their penchant for feeding off every detail of other people's lives, and the inherently ambivalent character of fiction, as of poetry and of drama, in that they are all alike a tissue of lies paradoxically constructed to arrive at unique truths. On a more directly personal level, he has occasionally referred to his own extremely emotional nature and suggested that the dispassionate character of his writing may have been an attempt to escape from the press of intense feelings by finding a distancing objective correlative for them. And he has also admitted to a baffled suspicion that writing may for him have constituted a form of escape – although from what precisely he claims never to have understood, except that he has never really felt completely comfortable in his own skin or confidently grounded in his own psyche.

Through Flint, Humphreys is able to explore objectively the danger that the artist may treat even friends and family as little more than raw materials, and may carefully arrange circumstances and surroundings to provide a satisfactory working environment. Flint admits to enjoying 'the comforts of living in Helen's flat, especially the room set aside for me to write'. (*HF*, 43) Real people can become the mere props of imagination, and a highly-developed imagination such as an artist may be said to possess can prove as dangerously active in real life as in the creative act. In *Hear and Forgive* it is a close call whether it is Flint or his girlfriend Helen who is the more prone to view the other through the distorting lens of the imagination. Each of them has a tendency to self-deception in the interests of self-satisfaction. And Flint has the additional advantage of being able to justify such convenient delusions in the name of obedience to conscience. As for the dangerous projections of one's personal dreams and ideals, the most vivid example of such in Humphreys's fiction occurs in *The Anchor Tree* where for the jaundiced middle-aged European academic Morgan Rees Dale all the supposed innocence of the New World is embodied in the form and person of the beautiful but unattainable young American, Judith Norrcop, who turns out, of course, to be very different from her worshipper's view of her – a view that is also, as the novel makes clear, itself rooted in a far-from-innocent sensual and sexual interest on Dale's part.

In some ways, then, Humphreys's view and treatment of the art he practises could be said to consist of a dialogue or dialectical relationship between two poles. On the one hand, he has undoubtedly absorbed the traditional Puritan view of fiction that has been transmitted to him by Welsh Nonconformity, according to which the novelist trades in deceit, is to be viewed with extreme caution, and is to be tolerated only for a capacity to communicate moral truths. On the other hand, Humphreys has spent a lot of his time in the company of actors and other such performers, and come to appreciate how profound dissembling on the stage can illuminate the human condition in utterly irreplaceable ways, whatever unfortunate traits of character it might encourage in life. Humphreys wryly noted of himself in a notebook entry from his early post-war London days, 'As a bizarre intellectual exercise you try to reconcile . . . left-wing reformism and practical nonconformity and keep in touch with Bohemia as well.' (CR, 87) He was thus recognising in his own artist-nature the same kind of strange duality to which his character Owen points when quoting from Montaigne in *The Little Kingdom*: 'We are I know not how, double in ourselves, so that what we believe we disbelieve, and cannot rid ourselves of what we condemn.' (LK, 155)

* * *

Of the spectacularly sudden twentieth-century collapse of chapel culture, Humphreys has written, 'the Welsh condition represented the spiritual crisis of the West in microcosm.' But he also saw in it a specific collective crisis of identity threatening a terminal collapse of distinctive Welsh nationhood, because for him ever since the late eighteenth century the life of the chapels had been the very lifeblood of a modern Welshness. Since so much of his fiction is concerned with the aftermath of Nonconformity's decline and eventual effective disappearance, it may be useful here to reflect on what is meant when reference is made to the Wales of the chapels in their nineteenth-century heyday as a 'Nonconformist nation'.

The development of Welsh nonconformity can be broken down into three phases. First, the establishment from the mid-seventeenth century onwards by such Puritan sects as the Congregationalists and Baptists of a marginal presence in a country that still obstinately clung to the Church of England. Second, the astonishing impact on eighteenth-century Wales of an evangelical Methodist revival that soon took on a very distinctively Welsh complexion thanks to several generations of outstandingly gifted leaders who prepared the way for Welsh Methodism's break from the Anglican church at the beginning of the nineteenth century – the first example since the Middle Ages of the creation of a separate, indigenous, Welsh institution. Lastly, the convergence of all of these denominations around the middle of the nineteenth century to form a common front that enabled the effective creation thereafter of a hegemonic working alliance of Nonconformists with enormous social as well as spiritual power. It was a power that soon extended into the political realm through Nonconformist support for the progressive wing of the Liberal party, so that Nonconformist Wales became politically radical Liberal Wales, and it was this powerful but also increasingly sclerotic alliance that delivered striking social, political and educational gains for the country and endured down to the First World War. But at that juncture misguided support of the Great War by some prominent Nonconformist ministers accelerated, if it did not actually precipitate, the rapid decline of chapel culture that heralded the equally rapid rise of Labour. It was a momentous politico-religious shift that was also a radical culture shift, since the power base of Nonconformity had been the traditional Welsh-speaking society of rural north and west Wales, whereas that of emergent Labour was the anglophone proletarian society of the industrial south-east.

This, then, is the world that is background to so much of Humphreys's fiction, even when it is not the foreground. He has been fascinated by the way the *mentalité* of Welsh Nonconformity – the distinctive structure and texture of consciousness it promoted – continued to permeate the secular thinking of twentieth-century Wales, informing intimate personal experience but also shaping social, cultural and political action. The messianism, for example, to which the Welsh people as a whole are prone – if latterly in its Socialist form – is a character trait that Hannah, in *A Man's Estate*, shares with Owen Richards in *A Little Kingdom* and Michael in *A Toy Epic*. Even the militantly atheistic young Communist Pen Lewis in *The Land of the Living* sequence is a believer in the utopian salvation of the proletarian masses, although not in sin. And as the hold of Nonconformity slackens, a new religion of sentimentalised sexual romance takes its place. No wonder that Prue, in the late novel *Gift of a Daughter* (1998), ascends the pulpit in a derelict chapel to sing a love aria from opera.

Humphreys has spoken of the *Iliad*, or epic struggle, between good and evil in the individual soul that Calvinistic Nonconformity promoted, and this is obliquely reflected in his work. The late, Gothic, short story 'Penrhyn Hen' features the grim story of Malan's vengeful care for her adulterous husband, now a helpless cripple, and her successful stratagem for ensuring her guilty sister, Sioned, is also trapped into becoming a carer. The incipiently liberal Sioned is thus drawn back into the dark religious culture of her natal world and ends by embracing a theology reconciling predestination and free will: 'We are as we are made and we are what we make.' (*GS*, 164) The loser in this incestuously intense and macabre Calvinistic *ménage à trois* is Sioned's partner, the hapless Bryn. His is a nature-loving, sentimental belief in forgiveness, in contrast to Malan's uncompromising belief in the wages of sin.

The trajectory of Welsh Nonconformity during the twentieth century has been carefully charted by Humphreys in many novels spanning his entire career, but most extensively in the seven-novel *Land of the Living* sequence. In the first of those novels, *Flesh and Blood*, we are introduced to the complexities of its history around the First World War. The rivalry between the denominations, the snobbish hostility between church and chapel, the suppression of women, the elevation of nineteenth-century Nonconformity to iconic status, the solidifying of the chapels into middle-class insti-tutions, the worship of social advancement and worldly success – all these and more are dramatically instanced. Several of the key features of the age are focused in the self-righteous personality and career of the increasingly egotistical and tyrannical Lucas Parry, the self-educated quarryman turned small-holder who struggles to become a minister – only for his denomination to reject him because of his lack of formal education – and his relationship with Esther, his wife, and their adopted daughter,

Amy. The likeable downtrodden Esther, skivvy and general dogs-body, has no illusions about Nonconformity past or present, secretly viewing it as patriarchally exploitative, which fuels young Amy's rebellious tendencies.

With the coming of the First World War everything changed, with chapel society torn between militant and pacific ministers. In *Bonds of Attachment* (1991), the sensitive young intellectual John Cilydd Moore is shown to have joined up partly to escape the clutches of his puritanical, overbearing grandmother. Psycho-logically disturbed and disorientated by his war experiences, post-war he can feel nothing but bitter anger at those who '"used to cheer the young men marching off, reading casualty lists like fat-stock prices"'. (*BA*, 250) It is such people as these who will now, 'with biblical protestations about God's will . . . patch up the broken pieces of the less worthy and the wicked that providence saw fit to exempt from the slaughter so that they can walk the world and possess it'. (*BA*, 273) His friend Val Gwyn shares his outlook, but is disturbed not so much by its spiritual as its cultural consequences, 'because for us [the Welsh people] the [Nonconformist] church is native, but the state is alien. We have no control over the state.' (*BA*, 266) It is a view shared by Humphreys.

The post-war situation is summed up in *The Best of Friends*, which opens with Amy – already aspiring to be a liberated woman of the new age of the 1920s – poised to throw her Bible, her uncle Lucas's gift, out of the train carrying her off to college. 'We are the people of the Book,' she exclaims scornfully, 'a chosen People.' (*BF*, 20) Implicit in her remark is a scorn for a people that has for far too long taken refuge in words, conveniently mistaking the power of the word for the real efficacy of the deed. As for her subsequent career, zig-zagging between different convictions and ideologies but always unwaveringly focused on achieving personal satisfaction and recognised social success, it typifies that of an unmoored people. Her views are counterbalanced by those of her gentle young friend Enid, steadfast in her belief that 'if we want to rebuild we can only do that on sound religious foundations.' (*BF*, 385)

Accordingly, the chapels began after the Great War to be home to theologically liberal and socially progressive ministers like Tom Arthog Williams and the eternal boy scout Tasker Thomas. They attempted to lead the remnants of the churches in directions of militant pacifism, remedial social action (which brought them into direct conflict with the new secular religions of Socialism and Communism, both of which rapidly gained ground in industrial south Wales), and politico-cultural nationalism. The latter cause emerges as a new, secular religion, and produces leaders like the saintly, self-sacrificial (or is it masochistic?) and gentle (or is it impotent?) Val Gwyn. He is irresistibly attractive to the idealist in the youthful Amy but lacks flesh and blood enough to satisfy her sensually and sexually in the way that the virile young South Wales miner and militant Communist Pen Lewis can. The latter's rejection of chapel religion is strangely mirrored in that of such creative young talents of Welsh-language culture as John Cilydd, a repressed homosexual who chafes under the intolerances and restrictions of traditional Nonconformity and ends up a tragic victim of his inner torments.

Insecurity, provincial suspicion, intolerance, xenophobia – during the Second World War Nonconformity falls victim to all three. Cilydd is hounded locally for his nationalist objection to the war, and his nightmare of cattle trucks, a flashback to his suffering in the trenches, is uncomprehendingly interpreted by his family as no more than guilt for not paying his chapel membership dues. Complementing Cilydd's traumatic recall is Tasker Thomas's touching public admission of how scarred he had been by his own experiences as padre at the front, and how they had turned him into a committed pacifist. Amy is driven as much by desire to escape from this moral quagmire as by raw ambition when she joins an international set of social intellectuals in London and begins her career as a Labour politician.

Following the Second World War, Nonconformity rapidly receded into the background of Welsh life. When Peredur, the son of John Cilydd, revisits the old family home, an old stonemason is dismayed that he doesn't know whether his family had been Baptist or Congregationalist. Yet even the atheistical Peredur yearns for the old certainties still faintly discernible behind 'mid-twentieth-century evangelical bohemianism and the well-meaning posers of Christian Aid and Third World concerts'. (*BA*, 119) His quest to discover the truth about his dead father is evidently a secular pilgrimage. It is therefore appropriate that his physical base is a sprawling, decaying old manse once belonging to the Annibynwyr and rescued from the clutches of an avaricious property developer. Peredur's moral drift is the common fate of many of Humphreys's post-war characters. In the short-story collection *Natives*, flame-haired Mel, who has left her chapel-centred rural village for the freedoms of the big city, tries to substitute romantic passion for her lost religious beliefs, but succeeds only in securing furtive liaisons with married men. Lonely, exploited and finally abandoned, she ends up committing suicide.

The morphing of religious belief into nationalist commitment that was also a prominent feature of post-war and post-Nonconformist Welsh society is disturbingly explored in *Bonds of Attachment* through the actions of Wenna, an attractive young chapel organist willing to countenance physical violence against property to advance her cause. 'We have to take into account this very sensitive Welsh nonconformist reverence for human life,' she concedes, before adding 'Okay, I don't mind. Blood has substance and meaning or I wouldn't be playing the organ in chapel when called upon, would I!' (*BA*, 342) Plans to blow up an electricity substation in an attempt to disrupt the 1969 Investiture of the Prince of Wales go disastrously wrong and Wenna dies in the resultant explosion.[8] The episode is one of many in which Humphreys, a conscientious objector on religious and nationalist grounds during the Second World War and a supporter of Plaid Cymru and Cymdeithas yr Iaith Gymraeg (both non-violent organisations), wrestles with the intolerable problem voiced as follows in *Bonds of Attachment* by John Cilydd:

There has never been a state of any shape or form in the history of the world that was not founded on bloodshed, not given its shape by violence and maintained by the cohorts of brute force in fancy dress. How can we ever be different? Wales of the [chapel] singing festivals and the white gloves? (*BA*, 273)

One of the most interesting products of twentieth-century Welsh Nonconformity to receive sustained attention in Humphreys's novels is what he himself has termed the Holy Fool. (*DPR*, 6) Like the Dostoevsky of *The Idiot*, he has been fascinated by the enigma of this phenomenon that is for him a consequence of the fact that 'the Protestant Reformation cracked the safe we called the New Testament, and like the spirits of Pandora's box the terrible ideas of justice, brotherhood, equality, love, freedom, service, have infected the whole of mankind and perhaps driven them mad.' (*CR*, 73) Nowhere in Humphreys's fiction are the implications of this more memorably explored than through the character of that reckless, crazy hero of the spirit, the mild-mannered J.T., in *Outside the House of Baal*, the supreme novel of Welsh Nonconformity, to be considered later in this study.

But J.T. does not stand alone in Humphreys's fiction. He lives in the company of others such as the Revd Curig Puw in the late novella *The Shop* (2005), whose commitment to his unworldly ideals leads first to breakdown, reducing him in the process to the pariah figure of a pathetic tramp, before he eventually becomes the community's unlikely hero. Tasker Thomas is another figure of this puzzling type – a reminder that those who might unkindly be termed 'wimps', ineffectual males such as Idris Powell in *A Man's Estate*, even Val Gwyn in the *Land of the Living Sequence*, all belong to the same brotherhood. The possibility of a sublimated homosexuality being involved is explored in the case both of Tasker (over whom, too, there hover suspicions of paedophilia) and of Bayley Lewis in *Outside the House of Baal*. The remark of J.T.'s son to his father in *Outside the House of Baal* – 'I don't think you've ever really forgiven me since I said Bayley Lewis was a homosexual' (*OHB*, 375) – is, however, not only an accusation of the homophobia lingering in even the most liberal of Nonconformist minds pre-war but also a disclosure of the embarrassed difficulties Welsh Nonconformity as a whole had with addressing any issues whatsoever relating to sexuality.

4

FICTION: FIRST PHASE

The Little Kingdom, the first of Emyr Humphreys's novels to be published, almost failed to reach a reader. Having completed the text, Humphreys managed to leave it behind on the seat of a train. That he succeeded in recreating it from working notes is, as he has observed, testimony to the obsessively intimate, intensely inward relationship a writer forms with any creative work in progress. And that the relationship should be a peculiarly intense one in the case of *The Little Kingdom* is not surprising because the novel is, in its unorthodox way, a kind of *roman à clef* in that it involves a fictional reworking of the incendiary incident at Penyberth that had set Humphreys on the road to becoming an *engagé* novelist.

What decisively distinguishes *The Little Kingdom* from the historical episode on which it is loosely based, however, is that it revisits the subject only to reproduce it in radically different terms and to re-enact it to radically different conclusions. Because whereas Humphreys has always been wholly approving of the action taken by 'the Penyberth three' – the utterly inoffensive and therefore highly unlikely trio of Saunders Lewis, Lewis Valentine and D. J. Williams[1] – the novel reflects on how, had the incident taken the form of violence not against state property but against an individual, the moral complexion of the act would have been totally altered, even though the motive behind it might have been as high-minded and every bit as legitimate in its cultural concerns as that underlying the action of the three nationalist arsonists. In today's terms, therefore, *The Little Kingdom* could be thought of as a species of 'alternative history', but in the form of a novel; a fictional exercise in a historical 'what if', or 'what might have been', undertaken with the view of dispassionately examining from a different angle the tangled complex of the moral issues that were implicated in the Penyberth action.

Humphreys's distanced and measured retrospective no doubt owed a great deal to the circumstances under which the text was written and the period in which it was completed. The novel's two vastly different places of origin are signified at the very end with the Joyce-like inscription: 'November 1943–November 1944: Caernarvon-Cairo.' Humphreys had therefore been working on the novel as the war in Europe was drawing to its end, a war of apocalyptic dimensions that had foregrounded the appalling human consequences of supreme dictatorial power. It is not surprising that Owen Richards, the glamorous young nationalist in *The Little Kingdom*, should become so intoxicated by the conviction that he has been divinely ordained to save his nation, that he does not even scruple to murder his maternal uncle, the grasping landowner Richard Bloyd, to prevent him selling land for the building of an aerodrome that could result only in the thoroughgoing anglicisation of the area.

The nature of the physical terrain that is under threat is sensuously rendered in the very opening scene of the novel that sees Richard Bloyd surveying his 'little kingdom':

It was a fine morning, but still chilly. Across the water he saw the Wirral emerge from the early morning mist; become once more a solid and substantial rich-green sea-girt land, speckled with red-roofed houses. The tide was out and down the estuary the mud flats gleamed in the oblique rays of the sun like the backs of enormous slugs resting in the low water. Down below on the water's edge the colliery's gaunt cranes emerged from a pall of mist and smoke, in its small harbour a dirty steamer blew its fog-horn into the silence, and after the silence was broken the day awoke. A train raced urgently across the coastal plain, as though all consideration was over, all decisions made, and the execution of plans begun. (*LK*, 5)

This, then, is the border country of Humphreys's own early years, a transitional zone in terms both of national cultures (the English

Wirral materialises as ominously looming backdrop to the Welsh scene) and of socio-economic processes: the Point of Ayr colliery leaves its mark on green countryside and estuarine marshland alike, while the straggling human settlement is obviously equally dependent on both. Implicit in the whole scene, therefore, is the issue of how far further the English society that has already crept across the border from the great industrial heartland of the Liverpool-Manchester conurbation should be allowed to spread. For Bloyd, of course, who sees only money when he looks at land, it is an issue that has already been conclusively decided.

The sensuous particularity of description that distinguishes this opening scene is a notable feature of a novel that is replete with such richly textured circumstantial observations: 'the thick briers twined over the old quarry like a torn blanket thrown over a hole. The fence was buried in high tufts of ungrazed grass, the posts broken and rotten, the wire brittle with rust.' (*LK*, 46) There is no telling here that this is the quarry to the bottom of which Bloyd will later be sent to his death by Owen. Equally striking are the casually telling observations of the body language of individuals, and nowhere is this more evident than in the description of the local councillors gathered in committee to discuss Bloyd's proposed sale of the aerodrome:

> In the centre of the room, erect as a toy soldier, Dr Cynhaeaf Price barked at Thomas Howells, who stooped over him like a study in ovals, his thick mouth shaped ready to thrust a resounding bass intrusion into the doctor's pizzicato. The doctor tapped his finger-nails with the pince-nez hung by a thick black ribbon about his neck, fixing his pugnacious stare towards Howells' pendant stomach, as though he were making a diagnosis. Herbert Herbert stood like a piece of stage property behind them, on the edge as it were, holding his hands on his meagre bottom, sometimes rubbing them up and down the shiny blue serge, never saying anything, moving his head like a spectator in a tennis match or a rare embarrassed bird caught at close quarters. (*LK*, 78)

Nowhere in Humphreys's later fiction does one encounter such a colourful richness of 'incidental' description. And if this is one prominent strength of *The Little Kingdom* another is the extra-ordinary dexterity with which, particularly in its early pages, the narrative inhabits and realises for us the utterly different and distinctive inner world of so many of the characters. The weakest aspect of the novel, though, is the melodramatic terms in which it renders the central character Owen's own mental processes. Even given that his megalomania means that he is tiresomely self-aggrandising and self-dramatising, the way in which these fatally dominant features of his personality are discursively rendered is somewhat overblown with the result that the agony of his moral struggle is compromised for the reader.

Humphreys does his best to offset this effect by showing that Owen's action arises from motives that are much more various and mixed than he himself is capable of realising, self-deluded as he is. But even here a certain novice crudeness and clumsiness is apparent, as when too obvious a parallel is drawn between the 'Welshy' Owen's youthful experience at English public school of being hurled (like the Biblical Joseph) down a pit and his action of propelling his uncle Richard Bloyd – whom he regards as similarly anti-Welsh – into the quarry. The novel's strength does not lie here, nor in its treatment of other prominent characters such as that of the ineffectual young Welsh poet Geraint Vaughan (the prototype of many such in the later fiction), nor in its handling of the love-triangle involving Geraint, Owen, and the local minister's beautiful young daughter, Rhiannon. Rather it lies in the narrative's ability to capture the very feel of a traditional form of Welsh life long gone by today, and already pretty far gone even in the post-war period in which *The Little Kingdom* is set. This culture is rendered with a lovingly detailed fidelity scarcely equalled by Humphreys even in his mature later fiction, where his main concerns in any case mostly lay elsewhere. And it is what continues to make this early novel such a precious, if flawed, achievement.

Several characters embody unsentimental aspects of this dis-appearing society, most notably the two old labourers, Siôn Bodlon and Tomos Bach, whom we first see muck-spreading, with 'thick sacks about their stooping shoulders; one wore a mud-caked pair of leggings, the other a new pair of yellow gaiters. Both wore clogs.' (*LK*, 123) 'Siôn had a reputation for talking. Tomos, on the other hand, hardly ever talked. His reputation was silence and thrift. Thrift was responsible for the absence of a bottom set of false teeth.' (*LK*, 124) They play the role of the rustic chorus familiar to us from the novels of George Eliot and Thomas Hardy, but here convincingly transposed to a thoroughly Welsh context. They are joined in their lugubrious ruminations by the much more aggressive young Tom Sion Sian, given to treating his mare as callously as he would his wife. Reckoned a good man with horses, 'He was a wiry man of thirty-three, red-haired, with weak blue eyes, a thick rather quarrelsome mouth, and long nose. His nerves were bad. He drank sweetened black tea without milk and made cigarettes from pipe tobacco.' (*LK*, 129) Towards the end of the novel, Tom, resentful of being laid off by Owen, joins other rowdies and toughs to disrupt an open-air political meeting organized by Plaid Cymru.

Other characters embody different features of this basically feudal, reactionary, peasant society. There is the dependent spinster, Miss Tudor, a retired schoolmistress wholly beholden to Bloyd for grudgingly allowing her to occupy the schoolhouse next to the Church School abandoned ever since the Nonconformists – fifty years earlier, before even the Boer war – had insisted on building their own non-denominational school to serve the largely chapel-going community. She hears Bloyd's car ominously drawing up outside: 'From the schoolhouse, Miss Tudor, chewing a piece of toast, peeped out between lace curtains, and drawing her shawl lightly across her narrow shoulders, came out to meet her landlord.' (*LK*, 7) The door having been left ajar, Bloyd glimpses within 'the pendant tassels of the red-plush tablecloth', and his nostrils pick up 'the warm animal odour that hung in the room' that Miss Tudor, breathless lover of Longfellow's poetry, occupies with her fat grey cat. (*LK*, 7) She is another relic of a bygone age.

There are also unattractive characters intent on adapting to the changing world around them, already evident in the built environment of the growing village. It features 'a blue-roofed nucleus of pre-war shops and houses, surrounded by the gay post-war expansion of red roof and plaster, spreading along the shore in small bungalows and ending among the green fields; tapering into uncompleted houses and unfinished avenues ending abruptly in mid-field.' (*LK*, 13–14) Those red tiles are by no means as innocently gaudy as they look. They are beginning to replace the grey Welsh slate traditionally used to roof houses, with the result that the great slate quarries of North Wales have effectively gone out of business, one by one.

One of the rodent-like characters that not only survive change but thrive on it is Cornelius Evans, local councillor, consummate fixer, would-be developer and small-time garage owner. His style of dress and whole demeanour evince his cunning appraisal of opportunities:

> Cornelius had long white hair and he wore a statesman-like wing collar, a black tie through a gold ring, and a rather greasy black suit. He handled the pipe and placed the nozzle in the petrol tank of the car with a pious sacerdotal air, and then stood, one arm raise above his head, a gold ring gleaming on his little white finger, until the operation was completed. (*LK*, 14)

All the time he is officiating in this way he is smiling ingratiatingly at the powerful local magnate Richard Bloyd.

Throughout the novel the change that is rapidly overtaking this community is effectively symbolised by cars and motorbikes, so it is no surprise that Cornelius should own a garage, even though he understands nothing about engines. Even the site of his garage, on the very edge of the expanding village, has been strategically selected, with Evans ensuring that he also owns the two fields either side. As for the garage itself, it is untidy, and full of grease and bits of cars: 'like a mechanical mortuary'. (*LK*, 178) A presage of things to come, it provides an ugly contrast, the novel implies, with the nearby Vale of Clwyd.

In the novel's dramatic conclusion, Owen is killed by Tom Sion Sian who has taken a job as watchman at the aerodrome, during the course of leading an attempted arson attack on the construction site. The epilogue is largely given over to the sad reflections of the elderly minister, the Reverend Morgan, who surveys the large bomber circling in to land with a mixture of sadness, resignation and yet quietly stubborn hope that love and kindness might after all be more than mere illusions, and that they might still be livingly operative in the world.

* * *

A Man's Estate is one of the most accomplished and arresting of Humphreys's early novels. Partly an examination of the morbid, decaying culture of the chapels during the first part of the twentieth century, its plot has, appropriately enough, a massive Old Testament quality but with something of the primal about it as well that brings classical Greek tragedy to mind. 'The ghost behind my novel *A Man's Estate*', Humphreys has written, 'was Orestes, the one who comes back and sees the old dispensation with unpitying objectivity.' (*CR*, 217)

Mrs Elis, a vengeful wife, murders her unfaithful husband with the tacit complicity of her secret admirer, Vavasor Elis. That gaunt suitor, a cousin of the deceased, subsequently marries her. Their sin is visited upon the children of both her marriages, Hannah and Philip having been born of her first union and Dick of her second. Indulged by his mother, the feckless Dick dies in the war, his death, like his life, a 'judgment' on his parents, and his story makes for 'a puny provincial tragedy'. And when the gruesome truth about the family history finally surfaces, their ageing mother escapes incontinently into wild madness while their mentally tormented and half-blind stepfather commits suicide. Philip is separated from Hannah at birth, they both remain virtually unaware thereafter of each other's existence. But the return 'home' of Philip following the removal of Mr and Mrs Elis from the scene marks the fateful culmination of his frustrated sister's long dream of the arrival of a saviour who will release her from the farm and the darkly brooding family that have long held her spirit captive. However, reluctantly returned to claim his 'estate' and a total stranger to this narrow cramped Welsh world, Hannah's brother Philip, Oxford academic, finds himself nightmarishly entangled, his journey back no better than a descent into a pit of 'Calvinistic sadists and hypocrites'. He duly departs again precipitously, abandoning Hannah to her pre-ordained fate. The atmosphere throughout is doom-laden; a judge-mental God hovers ominously over the scene; gloom seems to pervade every corner of the action. And the novel's meditation on the serpentine evils at the heart of human nature reminds us that it was contemporary with Golding's *Lord of the Flies*, and likewise very much a post-war novel full of ominous misgivings about core human nature.

Aspects of the novel's action therefore remind us strongly of the classic Calvinist belief not only in original sin but in predestination, albeit translated into twentieth-century terms. Thus, by the end, although Hannah has manifestly been in part the innocent victim of her mother's tyrannical grip on life, she also recognises herself to be irrevocably 'bound' to her mother and her step-father 'in the blood-cement of likeness. I have their coldness, their calculation, their trained hypocrisy, their perpetual misery, their unexpiated guilt.' (*ME*, 156) To the domestic fascism of everyday life on the family farm 'Y Glyn' she secretly adds her own fascist fantasy of supreme personal empowerment. Having begun as a victim of her circum-stances, Hannah ends up guilty of perpetuating the status quo; a feudal 'biblical' order grown rotten to the core. As for the tolerant post-Calvinist outlook of much of twentieth-century Welsh Non-conformity, that is ambivalently portrayed in the character of the young, well-meaning but malleable minister, Idris Powell. Devotee of a facile liberal theology of universal love, he crushingly discovers that he lacks the moral, psychological and spiritual resources to deal with the harsh realities of devious human existence. In contrast, 'murderer' and 'hypocrite' though the morally weathered and withered Vavasor Elis may be, in his daily implicit recognition of the severe Puritan values by which he will eventually be implacably judged, he possesses a compelling moral weight; a monstrous integrity.

'The artist', Humphreys observed his seminal 1953 essay 'A Protestant View of the Modern Novel' (collected in *Conversations and Reflections*), 'has shied away from the crude strength of the Protestant conscience – that constant, hoarse, dynamic whisper. But it possesses an exciting paradoxical combination of simplicity and complexity: an awareness of the great mystery, the infinite unconditional nature of God, and the egocentric solitude and sin of man in his trap of time.' (*CR*, 74) A core subject of *A Man's Estate* is the Protestant conscience, that stern guardian of a sense of personal responsibility. Many of the characters are urgently aware of being finally answerable for their own lives and actions.

The novel is a sustained study of the history of the Puritan conscience, its strengths and its weaknesses, in a period of moral confusion and uncertainty. That study covers a number of very different cases, ranging from that of the monstrously morally-deformed Vavasor Elis and his wife who finally fall tragic victim to the moral conscience that has worn their mind to tatters and their bodies to the bone, to that of the small garage owner Wally Francis, representative of a whole post-war generation that has scornfully turned its back on chapel values. In Wally's comfortably corpulent case, moral self-scrutiny has been turned into wily self-interest. Both he and his mistress, Winnie Cwm, display all the natural resourcefulness of predatory 'survivors', unlike Winnie's daughter, Ada, internally torn between conscience and heedless pleasure, who is only imperfectly able to turn her moral instincts into opportunistic amorality.

Humphreys's novel, then, specifically addresses the tensions within the dying 'Nonconformist nation' a century after its mid-nineteenth-century prime. And in this connection, it is useful to register the pivotal place *A Man's Estate* occupies in the development of the novelist. It was written some three years after his decision to return to Wales from London, and so Philip's similar journey 'home' allowed Humphreys to reflect obliquely on the ambivalent aspects of his own loyalty to a traditional culture and language under threat. The concept of 'rootedness' is one to which Philip, a sophisti-cated university academic and rational young scientist, gives short shrift, dismissing it as nonsensical superstition, 'unscientific neo-fascism'. (*ME*, 19–20) The novel, however, calls Philip's supposedly objective, 'scientific', outlook into question, exposing it as simplistic by indicating its compromised origins, in his case, in family and society. Meanwhile his sister, the claustrophobically cloistered Hannah, is helplessly aware of how the Elis family farm has remained in stubborn, decaying stasis while life in the surrounding Welsh countryside has been undergoing revolutionary change.

The nationalist convictions of Humphreys are likewise exposed to sceptical examination in *A Man's Estate*, not least in that Mrs Elis's version of that ideology is fanatical, chauvinistic and paranoid, a grotesquely pathetic echo of the brutally swaggering 1930s nationalism of Germany, Italy and Spain. As for Humphreys's internationalist convictions, these are evident in that he chose to fashion a Welsh 'family saga' suitable for obliquely exploring a Europe-wide post-war crisis: how to deal with a 'guilty', humanly destructive past; how to apportion 'guilt' in such morally opaque circumstances. There is a striking resemblance between the terms in which Humphreys recalled the experience of serving in Italy in the immediate aftermath of war and those used in the novel by a Hannah bewildered by her family situation. Her problem is that:

> I must somehow, out of myself like an industrious silk-worm produce the thread that will bind the fragments together, or lead me back through the labyrinthine wood of incidents behind whose apparently solid trunks sinister outlines seem to move in the dark. (*ME*, 48)

Humphreys used a similar image when recalling his post-war experience in Italy: 'in the terrible situation Europe was in at the time, we were moving around like children in the forest to a great extent.'

British fiction of the 1950s in general has recently undergone a positive revaluation, with critics now inclined to label it 'late modernist' or 'intermodernist', and to see it as engaging in a range of textual conversations with celebrated modernist predecessors.[2] The great modernist with whom Humphreys was most concerned at this time was William Faulkner, recently awarded the Nobel Prize for Literature. Humphreys was reintroduced to the great

American's novels by Edmund Wilson during the very period he was working on *A Man's Estate* and living, thanks to a Somerset Maugham award, in Salzburg. He immediately intuited that Faulkner's modernist innovations of style and expression had developed, as Robert Penn Warren had noted, 'out of . . . an anguishing research into the Southern past and the continuing implications of that past'.[3] Humphreys particularly valued Faulkner's genius for devising stylistic means of conveying the omnipresent, suffocating pressure of the dark past – felt even in the oppressive heat of the South – on the lives of his characters. Such a sense of the inescapable burden of cultural history and its modern encroachments corresponded to Humphreys's ambivalent sense of the significance for Wales of its inheritance: its Nonconformist 'estate'. The felt parallels between Humphreys and his Wales and Faulkner and his South are an important strand in the dense weave of *A Man's Estate*.

Humphreys also attributed his recognition of himself in Faulkner to the fact that both the Southern states and Wales were defeated 'nations', subsequently incorporated into the victorious alien state. The consequences of the defeat of the Confederate cause are everywhere, and obsessively, explored by Faulkner. One recurrent structural feature of his fiction is the contrast between the relics of the 'old order' – the impoverished, socially disempowered, and impressively flawed members of the cultivated classes that had traditionally sustained the ethos, the elaborate courtesies and the ethical codes of the antebellum South – and the creatures of the new order. The latter included the lower-class Southern whites who profited by allying themselves with this new 'foreign' culture of enterprise.[4]

Prominent instances of such base 'creatures' are the semi-literate and nakedly opportunistic members of the large Snopes family. They roughly correspond to the members of Wally Francis's clan and their associates who occupy a not dissimilar position within the structure of *A Man's Estate*. Their relationship to those decadent representatives of the old Nonconformist 'aristocracy', the Elis family, is broadly similar to that of the grossly fecund Snopes family to the decaying leadership of the old antebellum South. Hannah Elis disdainfully dismisses Winnie Cwm, Wally Francis and their promiscuously intertwined families as a 'low family scheming to rise'. (*ME*, 196) How, she asks herself, can she 'allow our family pride to be fouled by gutter people like Winnie Cwm and Frankie Cwm?' (*ME*, 197) She consequently refuses to acknowledge Winnie's daughter, Ada, as what in fact she is – her half-sister, born of a secret illicit union between Winnie and Hannah's father – and so fails to grasp the social and moral implications of the fact that they are both actually very closely related indeed.

The most dominant and memorable figure in *A Man's Estate* is Vavasor Elis, a candidate for tragic stature. He remains a compelling, if forbidding, figure because virtually alone among the main characters he is afforded the dignity of reticence. We are not admitted to his innermost thoughts and feelings until very late in the novel when he voices his suppressed inner torment through the heightened, measured, biblical rhetoric of public confessional prayer:

> Elis's lips trembled as they always did before he began. His eyebrows twitched rapidly. But tonight I noticed his head moved slowly from side to side as if he were rocking some crying sleepless grief within himself.
> 'Almighty and . . . Almighty . . . O Lord in the words of Cain, my punishment is greater than I can bear . . . year after year . . . from the day my eyes grew dim to this thou hast visited me with afflictions . . . Must I speak O Lord . . . Must I confess as a criminal still when I have accepted each affliction as a just punishment?' (*ME*, 393)

Even this climactic scene is carefully counterbalanced by an emphasis on the bathos of Vavasor's punctilious observation of the rituals of the prayer-meeting and on his affectingly uncoordinated, ungainly physical presence: 'He pushed open the door and sat down in the nearest seat exhausted, slowly removing the black hat he always wore to come to chapel. It was too big for him and almost rested on his large ears.' (*ME*, 393)

Elis is affectingly oblivious to the effect he is having on his listener. His semi-blindness emphasises his unconcern with social interaction and, in its way, figures his bleak self-arraignment. The weighty authority of the judgement he unsentimentally passes on himself is palpable: he is speaking not just of 'murder' but of mortal sin. There is a terrible fatalistic composure about him to the end: 'He hurried off towards the door as he always did as if he had endless business affairs waiting for his attention. "Good night now then," he said, as he always did leaving chapel.' (*ME*, 396)

At its end, *A Man's Estate* seems unable to imagine through Hannah, who has now, through the abdication of Philip, solely inherited her family's 'estate', both house and farm, a substantial, vibrant, living new future for the moribund, not to say morbid, Welsh nonconformist world of which she is the belated represen- tative. For any hint that such a future might nevertheless be possible, one must turn instead to the innocently ineffectual idealist Idris Powell, a young minister in faithful pursuit of Ada's love. Such an unconventional pairing might yet augur hope for the future of the chapels. But whereas the minister very evidently needs her, it is far from clear even to the spirited and mercurial Ada herself that she needs him – nor is it clear that, even should she accept him, such a union could possibly work and endure. In being entirely open-ended, or noncommittal, about the prospects of this relation- ship, the novel also concludes without resolving the question of whether there can be a future for Nonconformity or not. And so, *A Man's Estate* offers us no confident reassurance that its Wales has come to terms with its past and is thus well placed to face its future.

* * *

Published in 1958, the novella *A Toy Epic* continues to be the best known and most popular of Humphreys's works. It has remained on the Welsh schools' syllabus ever since I prepared an edition of it in 1989. In the year of its publication it was hailed in *The Church Times* as a 'minor masterpiece', and adjudged by *The Times* to be one of the best dozen books to have appeared in a year that had seen the publication of Boris Pasternark's *Dr Zhivago*, T. H. White's *The Once and Future King*, Mary Renault's *The King Must Die*, Angus

Wilson's *The Middle Age of Mrs Eliot*, and Iris Murdoch's *The Bell*. That year, too, it was awarded the Hawthornden Prize for work by an outstanding author under forty years of age by a panel including V. S. Pritchett and chaired by Lord David Cecil: past winners had included David Jones, Graham Greene and Siegfried Sassoon.

A Toy Epic had an intriguing composition history. It had first developed into an embryonic prose fiction having started life as a fragment of verse novel completed by Humphreys when he was very young and a conscientious objector. Following extensive reworking during the period Humphreys was working on the land near Caernarfon, it was next sent to Graham Greene, whom he had got to know when the already celebrated novelist published some early poems of his in *The Spectator*, and Greene expressed interest enough in it to encourage Humphreys to venture further. Accordingly, Humphreys next sent an expanded text to Greene at his new berth in Eyre and Spottiswood who noted his warm admiration for the core talent evident in it while regretfully noting that this expanded version of the text had in his opinion resulted in a diminution rather than an augmentation of its original power. A similar negative judgement was voiced by T. S. Eliot at Faber, whom Humphreys also consulted and further confirmed by Kate Roberts who went a helpful step further and explained, in diagram form, where the novel had gone structurally astray. Faced with such reactions and increasingly preoccupied with war work, he set the flawed text aside only to return to it more than a decade later when desperately searching for new material to broadcast when he was Head of Radio Drama at the BBC in Cardiff. A much shortened and intensively reworked text in Welsh went out over the airwaves as a short radio play for three voices (hence *Y Tri Llais*) in 1958 and was quickly published in novel form later that year. An English version of the same text appeared in print a few months later.

Given that the novella traces the 1930s journey from childhood through adolescence of three young characters (Albie, Michael and Iorwerth) in Humphreys's little corner of north-east Wales, it is not surprising that at this time he thought of himself as a 'north

Wales writer'. Having learnt Welsh, he had become aware that Mold, a few miles from Trelawnyd, had been home to the great nineteenth-century Welsh novelist Daniel Owen, and that E. Tegla Davies, a talented writer still active during Humphreys's youth, was a native of Denbighshire. Even more significant had been his discovery of Kate Roberts, a contemporary short-story writer of European stature, the native territory of whose creative imagination was the quarrying community of Gwynedd and the mountain fastness of Snowdonia.[5] His positioning as a writer from north Wales also stemmed in part from a wish to define himself against the 'south Wales school' of writers, mostly from Glamorgan, the most prominent of whom of course was Dylan Thomas. Broadcast on radio just a few years after *Under Milk Wood*, *A Toy Epic* can be seen as a riposte to that other, much more famous and influential, 'play for voices'.[6] But whereas Thomas's view of Wales was that of a self-professed 'provincial', the centre of whose world really lay in London, Humphreys was committed to nurturing through his work an awareness of Wales as a self-contained, multi-faceted nation with a long and complex history. The original *Times* reviewer shrewdly saw cultural distinctiveness as one of the novel's strengths: 'Small nationalities today are self-conscious in expressing and asserting themselves, and nothing could be more Welsh than . . . *A Toy Epic*, unless, indeed it were actually written in that language.'[7] Which, of course, it had been.

And it was not only in their respective attitudes to the Welsh language that Humphreys and Thomas differed radically. They also differed in their views of English. 'I was absolutely determined to avoid "Boyo English"', Humphreys has written. (*CR*, 192) It was a determination reinforced, by the mid-point of his career, by a respect for Wittgenstein's advocacy of minimalist expression[8] and for the great glories of the epigrammatically terse Welsh poetic tradition, as opposed to the garrulous oral tradition (partly deriving from the nineteenth-century Welsh pulpit) which lay behind the style of the inter-war 'Glamorgan School of writers' – whom Humphreys tended to anathematise as 'individualistic, iconoclastic and not really setting out to offer any kind of national expression'. (*CR*, 64)

But that said, *A Toy Epic* has in common with a south Wales work such as Thomas's *A Portrait of the Artist as a Young Dog* the intention of distilling the charged atmosphere of life in pre-war Britain. Both texts having in essence been written around the time of the Second World War, they are salvage operations mounted by the imagination, attempts to reclaim a lost personal and social world, and this lends them point and poignancy.

Tellingly, the boys' Grammar School days in *A Toy Epic* begin with an encounter with the faded sepia photograph of pupils killed in the Great War, and they end with the news of the young airman Jac Owen's death and with newspaper reports of troops massing for an armed offensive. The book constantly gives the impression of lives helpless before the might of historical forces, an inexorable fate prefigured in the collision between Michael's little car and a juggernaut bus towards the end of the novel. Moreover, the war is seen as being in part the outworking of other, more local, social tensions, such as were already ominously manifest in the class conflicts and confrontations with the military during the Great Strike of 1926 in which Albie's working-class father participates. As for Albie's particularly innocent and fearful young friend Iorwerth, he has premonitions of disaster as a boy when his 'quivering imagination' is startled by a road accident in the centre of town: 'In the twinkling of an eye, I was in the boy's dying place and I saw the blood rising inside me like quick-silver in a thermometer.' (*TE*, 57)

The *Times* reviewer in 1958 admiringly described *A Toy Epic* as 'a kind of three-part plainsong of the sublimated "stream of consciousness."' But it could equally well be described as richly contrapuntal in structure. Albie, Michael and Iorwerth come from very different social and cultural backgrounds. Albie is a council-house boy from the coastal town where all three end up attending Grammar School, and his parents have deliberately refrained from passing on to him the Welsh language they regard as a badge of inferiority. Michael is the son of a rector, who enjoys a privileged upbringing with a little 'Welshy' maid in attendance: he lives in a spacious vicarage with ample grounds where his mother fastidiously dons gloves to garden. Iorwerth is a thoroughgoing Welsh-speaking farm-boy, doted on by parents who end up being over-protective of their only son.

But then all three boys in their different ways have to struggle to come to terms with a dauntingly challenging adult world, having been hampered and partially damaged by their backgrounds. Socially advantaged as a son of the village vicar, but disadvantaged by parental neglect, Michael is a brittle compound of assurance and an arrogance that only masks a core insecurity. Accordingly he develops a messianic sense of personal 'calling' – in his case to become the saviour of the Welsh nation. The intense anxiety bred in Albie by the expectations his working-class parents have of his academic and social success sadly arrest and distort his development, leaving him psychologically broken and a self-perceived failure. And Iorwerth never remotely succeeds in breaking away from the smothering comfort of his close-knit family or of the narrow confines of the Welsh-language chapel culture to which he has from birth been confined. It is therefore little surprise that all three also find it extremely difficult to come to terms with dawning sexualities that have homosexual as well as heterosexual possibilities and that their relations with women are fraught and unsatisfactory. Add to this the fact that they clearly represent three sharply contrasting and highly significant aspects of the Wales of their time – most notably the country's deep class and cultural divisions – and one has some sense of that combination of wide scope with intensive focus that characterises this little novel, aptly entitled *A Toy Epic*.

The different phases of their development are subtly and economically registered, beginning in Iorwerth's case with his 'calf-like' growth 'from the semi-twilight of the darkened kitchen to the sharp light of the empty front garden'. As a little urban boy Albie by contrast runs 'from the shade of entry into the May sunshine trapped in our small square back garden', while later 'at three-and-a-half I played in the cul-de-sac, and numbers 13, 14, 15, 16, 17 and 18 stood on guard about me, watching me with square indifferent eyes'. (*TE*, 1) These houses may at first seem to be benignly protective guardians, but Albie's obsessive later use in adolescence of prison imagery alerts us to the likelihood that these houses seem to him by then to be grim warders already imprisoning his tender embry- onic ego. Iorwerth, on the other hand, never escapes from the cocoon of those early winter evenings around the cosy fire where his parents sit one each side 'like figures on a Christmas card'. (*TE*, 32)

Michael's upbringing would at first appear to have equipped him with all the social confidence necessary for survival and success as an adult. But the flaw in his own development is identified in adolescence by Albie's unappreciated and forthright girlfriend Ann who understands that 'really you know, deep down, he's a very cold person. He treats people as if they were all the same, all objects.' (*TE*, 118) But then his consciously 'well-bred' mother had always been hyper-anxious about observing the manners of the English middle-class, is always respectably reserved, avoids any display of maternal feelings, and employs a maid to look after the children. And his rector father, affable enough, is always remote and 'on duty' performing his clerical role. No wonder that Michael himself comes to feel his life on the brink of adulthood to be nothing but a succession of roles and masks.

In this novel, then, as in all his fiction, Humphreys implicitly acknowledges his indebtedness to Freud, while refusing the temp- tation to superimpose a 'master grid' of Freudian explication on what, his novella insists on demonstrating, is in fact the elusive and mysterious process of individual human development. The main subject of *A Toy Epic* is the mysterious process of constant change that constitutes the inner dynamic of human personality. It is appropriate that one of the books studied by the boys at County School should be Ovid's *Metamorphoses*. In the form of marvellously baroque myths of fabulous transformations, that book provides insights into the endless fluidity of the passional life that lies at the very heart of human existence. Also haunting the text are the wonder- stories of the *Mabinogion* so many of which contain episodes of shape-shifting.

Another of the novella's central preoccupations is that of Wales's colonial status, particularly evident in the plight of the Welsh language. To Iorwerth's bewilderment, the supervisor smirks when the boy asks to be allowed to sit the entrance scholarship papers in his native Welsh. The country lad is as yet too naive to realise that the state education system is the instrument deliberately used by the English government since the end of the nineteenth century to anglicise the whole culture – with the active support of the Welsh people who had been made ashamed of their supposed social backwardness. 'Bechgyn' says the mocking word over the boys' entrance to Llanrhos County School, but it could be better translated by a sentence echoing the inscription over the gates of Dante's hell: 'Abandon hope all ye Welsh speakers who enter here.' And Iorwerth's school experience is paralleled by his experience of listening in his Welsh chapel to an old preacher delivering a fervent jeremiad full of 'hwyl' in the grand nineteenth-century pulpit manner. Such sermons could be variously interpreted, as Humphreys was to write in *The Taliesin Tradition*, 'as the last desperate gesture of a people aware in their subconscious mind that their age-old faith was leaving them, or the first of a series of twentieth-century identity crises'. (*TT*, 195)

'There is a little Welsh Nationalism in *A Toy Epic*', wrote Maurice Richardson condescendingly in *The New Statesman* on the novel's first appearance, 'but nothing untoward.'[9] In fact, the state of the Welsh nation – as much in the 1950s when it was actually completed as in the 1930s when it was set – could be said to be one of the core concerns of *A Toy Epic*, and it is addressed most fully and frontally in the story of Michael. And he has something in common with Humphreys himself: both experienced a conversion to a nationalist faith at much the same age and they are pretty well agreed too in their analysis of the Welsh problem. In one way, Michael's espousal of the nationalist cause could be seen as a rebellion against his anglicised upbringing and his mother's background. But it could also be seen as a kind of acknowledgement of his Anglican heritage, because from the establishment of the Church of England in the Reformation down to the nineteenth century, Anglican clergy had played a very important and prominent part in the nurturing of Welsh-language culture. Yet by late Victorian times those same clergy, now English-speaking outsiders for the most part, had become no more than the mouthpieces of colonial control and the obedient servants of an anglicised and anglicising state.

Michael is also typical of the Saunders Lewis school of nationalists to which Humphreys likewise in part belonged in that not only does his political nationalism derive from a prior cultural concern but his imagination is fired by a twelfth-century poem by Hywel ap Owain Gwynedd.[10] In other words, his passion is not for the Liberal-Nonconformist Wales that Iorwerth represents, nor for the proletarian and proto-socialist Wales to which Albie belongs, but rather for an ancient 'aristocratic' Wales whose golden age was the Middle Ages. In effect, he opts to join the modern community of nationalist artists, scholars and intellectuals who had made the liberating and exhilarating discovery of a Wales whose cultural achievements were far more impressive and historically extensive than most of the contemporary Welsh with their 'colonised' imaginations were capable of imagining. He thereby realises that it isn't Wales that is narrow but rather his own ignorantly limited conception of his country. But his education isn't complete until he visits a political conference and recalls the 'history and significance of the castle'. (*TT*, 103) Then his vision grows militant as he realises that in order to survive not only will Wales have to resist current historical forces, she may also have to mount a counter-attack and take History by storm. However, Michael becomes dangerously intoxicated by his sense of mission, and Humphreys is careful to distance himself from his final ambitions.

'The struggle of man against power is the struggle of memory against forgetting', wrote Milan Kundera.[11] One way of reintroducing a nation to its own forgotten history is through providing it with conscientiously accurate but compelling historical fiction. Emyr Humphreys has devoted most of his long writing life to doing precisely that. Indeed it can now perhaps be seen that *A Toy Epic* is itself intended to function as an aide-memoire for a nation, short though it is. It is thus very much one of Humphreys's most important and unforgettable contributions as novelist to his Wales's continuing struggle for survival.

* * *

One evening in the 1960s, while driving his elderly mother home, Humphreys was startled by a remark she made as she gazed through the windscreen: 'It's bad luck to look at the moon through glass.'[12] It made him realise she was a survivor from a lost age. And in part out of his sudden urgent wish to place on record aspects of that world his mother had known came *Outside the House of Baal*, Humphreys's single greatest work and his most impressive attempt to calibrate the changes that had drastically altered the Welsh landscape during the first sixty years of the twentieth century.

In the novel he skilfully interweaves two distinct narratives and timelines. The first is confined to a single day in the early 1960s in the life of an elderly couple: J. T. Miles, a dreamy, mild-mannered, retired minister, and his crabbily practical sister-in-law, Kate. The second spans some six eventful decades, from the closing years of Victoria's reign down to the novel's present, and, by tracing the extensive network of events and relationships that have constituted the life-experiences of J.T. and Kate, it succeeds in offering a compelling, ambitiously inclusive portrait of Welsh social, cultural and political history during a period of turbulent changes that included two world wars and a great economic depression.

1961 saw the very belated repeal in Wales of the Sunday Closing Act that had been a mainstay of the alcohol-free Welsh chapel Sabbath since 1881. This victory of pub over chapel, which also meant the end of a distinctive Welsh way of life, is implicitly addressed in a novel in which the triumph of the values represented by the raucous, vulgar public house (figured in the novel as the House of Baal) marks the final decay of Welsh Nonconformity. This is an issue whose implications are richly problematised in the novel, most particularly through the ambivalent career and character of J.T., who seems to exist permanently at the very point where different judgements come most hauntingly into conflict. The motherless son of a secret drunkard given to sporadic violence, J.T. defies his early background by becoming a painfully conscientious young minister of controversially liberal theological beliefs and outspoken critic of the First World War. With his wavy hair and film-star good looks the shy, impressionable young man, intensely aroused by sexual passion but baffled by it, would seem to be the perfect match for the vivacious, rebellious and uninhibited Lydia, Kate's sister, who is desperate to break free of her early life on a farm tyrannically dominated by her father. But their marriage founders on their contrasted temperaments and his increasingly impractical conduct in the name of his spiritual beliefs. Charmed at first by his idealism, she grows impatient and then bitterly resentful of the damaging consequences for her and their children of what seems to Lydia to be his sheer self-indulgence and self-absorption. Their relationship is one of many through which Humphreys examines the collision between the decline of Nonconformity and the rise of the New Woman.

Lydia's reactions are mirrored by many who encounter J.T. They divide into puzzled admirers of his impossibly high standards and prominent selflessness, and those who are sceptical of the authenticity of both, or angrily resentful, like Lydia, of their destructive effect on others. To the very end, he remains a great enigma, the Gordian knot of whose character can never be untied. By centring on him, *Outside the House of Baal* attains the stature of a tragic elegiac meditation on a whole vanishing culture, all the more impressive and authoritative because it does not flinch from embracing a range of characters and situations that reveal the seedy, unsavoury, and downright ugly aspects of the chapels. Drunkenness, sexual hypocrisy and moral dishonesty, petty tyranny, meanness, avarice, social ambition, self-deception, sexual inhibition, sexual abuse, bigotry – all these and more are laid at the feet of the chapels.

Nor is J.T. himself immune from constant, suspicious scrutiny in the light of all of this. Is he selfless or selfish, guileless or manipulative, creative or destructive? The questions are insoluble and tease us out of thought. The very process of reading provokes internal debate of a radical kind that tilts the axis of our customary value judgements, forcing us to ask searching questions of ourselves. There is nothing clear-cut about J.T. and his web of relationships. His maternal grandmother regards her little 'Joe Miles' as unconsciously cunning: seeming weak, he always succeeds in getting his own way. Lydia's autocratic, grimly puritanical father declares him roundly to be an incompetent idiot; J.T.'s sister-in-law, the indomitably practical Kate (Sancho Panza to his Don Quixote),[13] tartly deplores his readiness 'to be nice to everybody' (*OHB*, 90); her graspingly materialistic brother, Dan, is even more severe when, in his senility, he impatiently calls him 'an old fool' to his very face.

So many of J.T.'s presumably well-intentioned actions result in disaster not for himself but for others. Stubbornly insisting on setting out to save a wounded soldier stranded under enemy fire in no man's land, he gets his companion stretcher-bearer killed; intent on sacrificing his salary to show solidarity with the striking miners when a minister in the industrial valleys during the great Depression, he virtually starves his wife and children out of house and home and seriously endangers his marriage; magnanimously preparing to forgive his exasperated wife for what he suspects is her adultery, he succeeds only in driving her away. As a First World War pacifist, J.T. courageously heckles a rabble-rousing, war-mongering politician (clearly modelled on Lloyd George), but it is his soldier friend Griff who has to rescue him from the clutches of the police and the local thugs as they start to beat him up.

When we first encounter J.T. he is an old man waking up in the morning and viewing the grey world through the golden haze of the bedroom curtain. Many would see that as an expression of his escapism, his lifelong lack of realism; but then he claims to live by a definition of reality entirely different from the ordinary and obediently attuned to the Gospel. He is an obstinate believer in the hidden, unrealised goodness of the whole of human kind. An incorrigible, and in many ways an intolerable, spiritual extremist to the very end, he wagers everything – even his very life – on his beliefs, but in the process implicates others willy-nilly. Passing judgement on him, we readers inescapably reveal the values and choices on which we are gambling our own lives. The novel thus brings us to an uncomfortable knowledge of ourselves. To J.T. may be applied the remark made of a character in another of Emyr Humphreys's novels, *Unconditional Surrender* (1996): 'It would be a relief to be rid of the young man and his over-active conscience.' (*US*, 119)

J.T. is viewed with suspicion not only by society at large but by his own denomination because of his liberal, socially progressive beliefs. His First World War pacifism is unacceptable not only to conservative Calvinist bigots like the weaselly little deacon, Jac Brain, but to the eminent principal of his own theological college. His fellow students, precociously wise to the ways of the world, treat him with amused contempt. To Lydia's growing horror and disgust he finds refuge only in the economically devastated and politically turbulent south Wales valleys where his ministry can assume the crusading social forms that satisfy his conscience but blight his family's life. His allies are agitators, oddballs and mavericks. Rejecting the dogma of original sin, as he'd rejected the dogma of the Immaculate Conception, he outrages the orthodox by replacing their God of retributive justice tempered by unpredictable grace with his hungry advocacy for a God of universal love – the kind of love, one might note, of which 'little Joe' himself had been so conspicuously starved as a boy.

His helpless, impractical nature may move women to mother him, but they often find themselves trapped in a relationship they find irritating or worse. Late in life his daughter, Thea, keeps him affectionately at arm's length, leaving the increasingly heavy duty of care to Lydia's exasperated sister Kate, once a young secret admirer of J.T. and still, perhaps, grumblingly fond of him in ways which her puritan nature prevents her from admitting. Conspicuously refraining from judging others, he ends up hearing that his son, Ronnie, has been made to feel inadequate all his life by his father's unconsciously demanding moral stature; the success at Oxford that J.T. so resents on cultural grounds has therefore been his son's way of gaining self-esteem. Everything that J.T. does seems subject to the law of unintended consequences.

Time's verdict on him is also cruel. An exceptionally moving scene is the one where a J.T. driven to the edge of emotional breakdown by the insufferable dawning of a nuclear age, struggles with the new technology of a tape recorder to send a tearful message to distant relatives in North Dakota. Much more than his trials with the machine, the real obstacle to communication between generations is the dated language into which J.T. automatically lapses, as he is painfully aware:

> We are all bound into the same family by the bonds of love. You know I am a preacher so you will not blame me for preaching . . . Just as the distance between us is annihilated by this device and I am speaking now in your hearing, so it is with the means of salvation that quicken our lives with purpose and with meaning . . . (*OHB*, 382)

Words fail him as he is overcome with emotion. But words fail the ageing J.T. in any case, as he repeatedly discovers that his language no longer has any meaning. A brashly importunate seaside photographer armed with a pigeon as a prop, fails to understand J.T.'s allusion to the dove of the Holy Spirit. Yet he struggles to persist in forgiving a morally, culturally and spiritually errant Wales, just as his favourite prophet, Hosea, had forgiven his adulterous wife.

Somehow he survives: the last glimpse we have of him being, appropriately enough, as he sets out to book a mystery tour of north Wales – the very place where he was born. Nor does J.T. provide the only example in the novel of how to survive, to outlast not just one's generation but the society that has formed, and continues to inform, you. The most powerful example is offered by Kate, with her simple, stubborn, effortful persistence in the labour of mere living. In her grumpily pragmatic way, she exhibits a toughness, a resilience, a resourcefulness and even a degree of adaptability, that is foreign to the unbending J.T. And the novel ends with her preparing for an outing with her niece, Gwyneth, with the characteristic words: 'Got to have the address or we won't know where to go.' (*OHB*, 398) With his preacher's eye for an allegory, J.T. would undoubtedly have placed a metaphysical meaning on that sentence, and the novel, too, has primed us for that possibility. But for the practical Kate, whose religious belief has long dwindled away to a mere vague hope that life's meaninglessness may after all reveal some hidden purpose some day, the sentence means no more than it says.

In its magisterial, challenging, moving and inimitable way, *Outside the House of Baal* remains the major fictional work of Welsh Nonconformity and it is, perhaps, the most outstanding English-language novel to have come from Wales to date. It is proof that the comment made by Aled in *Gift of a Daughter* is one that applies to Emyr Humphreys's heart as a novelist:

> After all I had, so to speak, an inside knowledge of the decline and fall of Welsh nonconformity: of the strength and weakness of a way of life that had in some sense been the high-water mark of community strength and civilization of this corner of the globe. (*GD*, 34)

And in being an elegiac celebration of that way of life, the novel is not entirely undeserving to be ranked alongside other great classics of the melancholy memorialisation of a culture, such as Robert Musil's *The Man Without Qualities* (1930–43), Joseph Roth's *The Radetzky March* (1932), Allen Tate's *The Fathers* (1938), Giuseppe Tomasi di Lampedusa's *The Leopard* (1958) and the seven novels about Yoknapatawpha County by William Faulkner.

* * *

While working on *Outside the House of Baal*, Humphreys began to contemplate a different, complementary, way of encompassing in fiction those features of Welsh history during the twentieth century that most engrossed him. He outlined the growth of this idea as follows:

> I began in 1969–70 with the intention of a large, 'broad' novel that would attempt to achieve in Space what *Outside the House of Baal* had achieved in Time . . . A note I wrote at the time reads like this: 'The novel is meant to be a companion to *Outside the House of Baal* working laterally in space instead of linearly in time . . . The novel should be shaped comment on contemporary life that springs from the history of twentieth-century Wales . . . the Mother (i.e. Amy) is most important because she represents the historic thrust from poverty to affluence, from chapel to atheism, from revolution to neo-royalism – the compulsory heir of the historical process. (*private correspondence*)

The novel that resulted was *National Winner*, which does indeed introduce Amy to readers, but only at that period in her life when she has already become Lady Brangor and is grandly holding court at Brangor Hall, to the discomfort of her youngest son, Peredur. To Amy's intense irritation, he becomes obsessed with the past she herself is so very anxious to forget. In particular, he is neurotically concerned to establish the real reasons for the suicide of his father, the solicitor and gifted Welsh-language poet, John Cilydd, idol of a culture Amy herself has long since impatiently abandoned.

In writing the novel, Humphreys came belatedly to realise that it would not, after all, allow him the licence and latitude he had so much wanted to range freely over many locations and decades. Consequently, he decided to embed *National Winner* in what became a seven-novel sequence with the eventual composite title of *Land of the Living*. All six of the other novels were published in the chronological order of their respective narratives, with the originally freestanding *National Winner* now slotted – rather anomalously, given its distinctive style, somewhat unfocused structure and relatively small cast of characters – into its chronological place as the sixth and penultimate novel in a completed sequence: *Flesh and Blood* (1974), *The Best of Friends* (1978), *Salt of the Earth* (1985), *An Absolute Hero* (1986), *Open Secrets* (1988), *National Winner* (1971), *Bonds of Attachment* (1991).

Attention has already been paid in this study to some of the leading themes threading together the novels in this septet, as also to the original cat's cradle of intense relationships between a number of suggestively contrasting characters – the ambitious Amy, raised in poverty but educated out of her original peasant class at university; her young friend, Enid Prytherch, idealistic Welsh nationalist who dies young giving birth to Bedwyr; Enid's husband, John Cilydd, repressed homosexual and *poète maudit* who disastrously marries Amy on the rebound after Enid's death; Val Gwyn, gentle and good-looking, a Welsh nationalist and internationalist who enchants the impressionable Amy for a period but proves both psychologically and physically incapable of capturing her; and Pen Lewis, the virile young miner who, as a Communist, is an

Internationalist of a different stamp and is killed in Spain, but not before becoming Amy's passionate if unreliable lover and begetting a son, Gwydion.

Gwydion the film-director, every bit as cheekily unpredictable and ingeniously plausible as his namesake, the devious wizard Gwydion in the *Mabinogion*, is the polar opposite in character to the successful architect Bedwyr, adopted by Amy after Enid's death, who – again as his Arthurian name ('Bedivere') suggests – is solid, decent and upright to a fault, just like his biological mother. As for Amy's third child, Peredur, a failed young academic, he takes after his father in his gaucheness and lack both of social skills and of physical attractiveness. And like his famous namesake – the Percival of Arthurian Romance – he becomes fixated on a quest for a holy grail, in his case the truth about the violently tempestuous relationship between his ill-suited parents and its tragic outcome in his father's death by his own hand. From *National Winner* onwards, therefore, the final novels in the sequence track the playing-out of the fraught interrelationships between this trio of brothers, two of them sleek with executive success but the third a hopeless loser and misfit, and their relations with their endlessly compelling and shape-shifting mother, the indomitable Amy.

Amy was, after all, ever reluctant to become a mother – her two pregnancies were both unintended, and her adoption of little Bedwyr could obviously not have been foreseen. Moreover, her childbearing and childrearing had cost her dearly –the unwanted arrival of poor little Peredur even prevented her from being adopted as a parliamentary candidate in a highly winnable seat, so that the little boy was resented by her from birth. No wonder Amy's last words to each of her sexual partners before intercourse had invariably taken the form of a haplessly unavailing plea: 'Please be careful.' Indeed, one of Humphreys's major intentions in *The Land of the Living* was to dramatise the plight of women in twentieth-century Welsh society right down to the dramatic and revolutionary advent of the pill. Time after time they are shown to be the victim both of biology and of patriarchy – the latter successively embodied in the overwhelmingly male Nonconformist establishment, the worlds of medicine and academe, and the dominant sociopolitical order.

And while Humphreys has several times adversely compared the status of women in Wales during the past century with their standing under the old Welsh laws of Hywel Dda[14] and the respect afforded them in ancient Celtic society, the immediate stimulus to his extended treatment of the subject was probably his early awareness of his mother's situation. A singularly high-spirited, independent and intelligent woman, she ended up effectively tied to home and family, raising not only a son of her own but also (like Amy) an adopted son, left after her sister had died in childbirth. In her, Humphreys could discern the frustrated lineaments of the New Woman, that scandalously exotic creature that suddenly appeared after the First World War, albeit in strikingly different guise, in the Soviet Union, the USA of the Jazz Age, and even the sedate English shires. This new being alarmed so many men – including Humphreys's mentor Saunders Lewis, whose great verse-drama *Blodeuwedd* is a memorable meditation on the phenomenon.[15] One of the most liberating instruments and symbols of the New Woman was the bicycle, and in *Flesh and Blood* the schoolgirl Amy is repeatedly shown to revel (rather poignantly, given her future) in free-wheeling down the hill from the little upland homestead of Swyn-y-Mynydd, the wind intoxicatingly winnowing her hair.

Amy has been primed young for rebellion because she has seen in close-up the way her beloved adoptive mother, Esther, has been brow-beaten into meek submission by her demanding, overbearing and self-pitying husband, Lucas. Alas, Amy's early bosom friend, Enid, a cosseted member of the Welsh bourgeoisie, has undergone no such educative experience and so, gentle soul that she is, the intellectually gifted Enid allows herself to be overcome by pity for the abject incompetence of John Cilydd and to be overawed by his poetic genius. She accordingly marries him, intent – like Dorothea in *Middlemarch* – on nothing but complete, self-abasing, devotion to her husband's service. It is a form of suicide, so it is hardly surprising that the ill-starred marriage results in a difficult birth that leads to Enid's death from puerperal fever, due to the inadequacies of a male-dominated medical system with a callous disregard for the needs of women. And Amy – in what is at once a misguided tribute to her dearest friend, an act of female weakness and a boldly defiant gesture of sisterly solidarity – accepts responsibility for the raising of Enid's child. Morally admirable though it is, it is also yet another trap of a kind, another reminder of the double-bind in which women seem inexorably trapped, and an undeniable obstacle to Amy's development into a truly free spirit.

Whatever, then, the strong reservations implicitly registered throughout the *Land of the Living* sequence about the trajectory of Amy's social and political career that sees a young Welsh nationalist end up comfortably co-opted by the English establishment and an idealistic Socialist revelling in all the baubles of capitalist production, her case is also always sympathetically viewed against the complicating background of humiliating early poverty and original imprisonment within a claustrophobically narrow male environment. Humphreys deftly manages to render all his characters ultimately somewhat enigmatic by deploying a narrative technique that involves building a novel out of a sequence of cross-referring brief scenes or tableaux, each of which offers a sharply delineated but deliberately 'shallow' interaction of characters and competing ideologies. This allows for rapidity of movement over space and time, and promotes a highly suggestive dialogue between scenes, but it also prevents any in-depth analysis of psychologies.

With the sole exception of *Bonds of Attachment*, the final novel in the series, the texts allow us to know characters only by what they say and do, and through what others say about them – although it could be argued that this objectivity is more apparent than real as rarely is it difficult to discern where the author's sympathies primarily lie. There are also deliberate lacunae generated by a narrative structure which is more a collection of snappy short stories than a single continuous narrative. At first, such is the articulacy of the characters that they seem to be in full and conscious possession of themselves. But gradually inconsistencies and ambiguities quietly emerge that undermine the certainties of our initial assessments – and, more importantly, that call the ideologies with which the speakers themselves so eloquently identify into question. The novels thus function not as the vehicles or mouthpieces of ideologies but rather as the sceptical inquisitors of ideologies: they implicitly draw attention to the telling distinction between the overt and covert explanations of why people do things. Readers may also find themselves resorting to ideological models – such as Freudianism – that are *not* mentioned in the texts to remedy the deficiencies of those which are so vociferously paraded.

At one point in the novel – which is also the low point of her career – Amy's life briefly threatens to assume a tragic complexion. In the period covered by *An Absolute Hero*, she has already embarked on her initially erratic progress across the ideologically fractured social and political terrain of Wales. She has moved hopefully out from her pinched early environment into a broader Welsh world, only to blunder into its cultural divides before falling victim to the verbose ideological disputes by which the Wales of the 1930s is hopelessly riven. But while already becoming aware of how her early background in poverty means she is naturally attuned to the international socialist gospel being preached by Pen Lewis and others in the otherwise foreign valleys of Wales's industrial south, she continues to trust primarily to the politico-cultural compass that is provided by the two closest to her, Enid and Val. But then both suddenly die, leaving her adrift and trying fruitlessly for a time to take her bearings from her loyal memories of them.

In *The Historical Novel*, Georg Lukács famously argued that the conditions for tragedy occur when, at a given historical moment, the contradictions that have been developing in the general social milieu are internalised and thus fatefully woven into the very fabric of private individual character.[16] So it is with Amy at this point, and so the novel becomes haunted by images of her seeking refuge in a garden shed only for a 'stack of earthenware plant pots' to tumble over, so that 'the dust made her cough' (*AH*, 37); of her desolately wandering the amusement arcades of Llanelw; of her gazing out of the window at damp and mildewed Glanrafon and seeing 'an ancient swing and beyond it an unkempt wisteria drooped along a high brick wall' (*AH*, 15); and of a morning at Cae Golau when a sparrow perches 'on the edge of a mildewed boot without laces that must have belonged to Cilydd's great-uncle', and gives her 'a sharp malevolent glance before taking off'. (*AH*, 159)

But as the remaining novels in the sequence proceed to make unequivocally clear, Amy is one of History's survivors – although whether born so or made so by her early environment is left deliberately uncertain. She has a sixth sense for the direction in which the future, and with it her own eminent prosperity, lies. Consequently, as she slowly recovers from the death of her young nationalist friends at a young age, a shocked and saddened Amy comes to realise that theirs was ever but a lost cause. Thereafter, she sets her sights determinedly on London and success, although not before injudiciously saddling herself both with a baby and a wholly unsuitable first husband, both of whom become for her unwelcome spectres from her past. The return of what she has repressed is, however, manifested most unattractively and intractably in the form of her ugly duckling of a son by John Cilydd, Peredur, every bit as tormented a soul as his father had been.

As for the hyper-sensitive poet-solicitor John Cilydd himself, his is one of the most complex and compelling of the portraits by Humphreys, in the vast gallery of his fictions, of psychically-maimed representatives of a Welsh-language culture the saving of which is thereby implied to depend on a prior process of psycho-social healing. Peredur's quest for the truth about the tensely destructive relationship between his parents therefore comes to resemble Sir Percival's search for the Holy Grail that is in the keeping of the Wounded Fisher King. Traditionally represented as wounded in the groin, the Fisher King is as unable to beget the future as he is to minister to the needs of his own stricken lands. Some of the later versions of the story have two wounded protagonists – the King and his Son, who is slightly more proactive than his father, as of course is the stubborn, if unprepossessing young Peredur.

Many of Humphreys's ostensibly realistic later novels are based on this kind of relatively hidden and secret substructure of Welsh legend and myth that can be accessed – and thus in a sense activated – only by readers sufficiently committed to fully understanding the implications for Wales of these fictions as to take the trouble to acquire the relevant cultural knowledge. Similar use is made of references to incidents and personages from Welsh history and to classical Welsh-language texts. Thus 'Argoed' – the name of Kate's family farm in *Outside the House of Baal* – is an allusion to T. Gwynn Jones's great poem of that title.[17] And behind the character of John Cilydd hovers the faint ghost of Prosser Rhys, the pioneering Welsh homosexual poet of the interwar period.

John Cilydd is brought into focus only in the final novel of the sequence, *Bonds of Attachment*, and all because of a traumatic incident experienced by Peredur when he was barely eight: hearing his mother's high scream of anger, he looked up from play to see a white-handled carving knife hurtling through a window to the sound of breaking glass, and his father's 'face as pale as a ghost beyond the jagged edges of the shattered glass before he disappeared from my sight for ever'. (*BA*, 29) Determined to get to the bottom of this event, Peredur begins by gaining privileged access to the diaries and notebooks his father left behind, all crammed full of his 'small, secretive handwriting'. (*BA*, 49) Very gradually he begins to piece together the story of his father's life, as the notebooks range over the suicide of John Cilydd's frustrated sister, Nanw, by fire, his anguished wrestling with his poetical gifts, his training to be a solicitor in a firm proud of its allegiance to king and Empire, his dawning disgust at the chapels' preaching of War, his debasing, psychologically disfiguring experience of the trench warfare into which he had been so reluctantly initiated as an innocent 'seventeen-year-old . . . carrying his chapel upbringing with him like the down on his cheeks' (*BA*, 48), and his unbearable lifelong suffering thereafter 'on a barbed-wire cross'. (*BA*, 48) Also confessed to in these notebooks' pages are the unfaithfulness of John Cilydd's second wife Amy, the rapidly growing antagonism between the unhappily married couple, and his own bashfully gay flirtations with handsome young opportunists like Eddie or the hapless Ken Lazarus.

Peredur's guide through this labyrinthine underworld of his father's strange, secret and distant past is Hefin Mather, the librarian who for Peredur seems to assume the guise of a latter-day Merlin and is the nerdy keeper of the Welsh nation's ancient mysteries. Complementing these researches is his subversive scheming – with its dangerous undercurrent of violence – to disrupt the 1969 Investiture of the Prince of Wales at Caernarfon Castle. This results in a passionate emotional entanglement with Wenna Ferrario, a pious young chapel organist who has been convinced that the desperate plight of Wales calls for equally desperate measures. Her reckless lawbreaking exploits result in her blowing herself to smithereens in a botched attempt at blowing up an electricity sub-station.

As for that previous episode of violence that had so traumatised Peredur when a boy and precipitated his father's suicide, it turns out to have been triggered by John Cilydd's impulsive pledging of half his income to a Peace movement, an action that had roused Amy to such a fury that it found exasperated expression in her hurling of the knife. It is, of course, Amy, too, who inevitably has the last word both of this novel and of the sequence as a whole. And as was only to be expected it turns out to be as insinuatingly ambiguous as her whole life. On her death bed, she beguiles the defenceless Peredur with the suggestion that he assume responsibility for the future running of Brangor Hall – that ancient pile he has so despised as the sign of the ill-gotten wealth and high English social status his mother has worked so assiduously to acquire. And in a last, melodramatic gesture, cunningly addressing Peredur as 'your father's son', Amy even offers him the illusion of a freedom to choose whether to accept this responsibility or not:

> Her hand was in mine. She was thin. It had begun to shake. She had taken off her rings. They slipped off too easily. I lifted her hand to my lips and kissed them. What else could I do? (*BA*, 357)

* * *

While halfway through his *Land of the Living* sequence, Humphreys briefly switched to writing a slim novella, *Jones*, elegantly blending social comedy with a subtly cumulative pathos. Published a few years after the 1979 Referendum on Devolution had resulted in Wales in a devastating majority in favour of the status quo and thus against even the most modest degree of self-government, the novel focuses on Goronwy Jones, a lecturer in Geology at a Teachers' Training College, who has long since settled in London and turned his back on his Welsh roots. These lay in the arid landscape of a hill farm where his hard-fisted father had practised subsistence farming and periodically shut him up in the pig-sty as punishment for some minor misdemeanour. But now, at the age of fifty-seven and on the brink of voluntary early retirement, Jones finds himself involuntarily and most unwillingly bringing his earliest memories and experiences to mind as he attempts to assess the sum meaning and worth of his life in unsparingly honest perspective.

Jones is a miniature masterpiece and, like so many of Humphreys's novels, it centres in part on the continuing fatal allure of London for the Welsh, and on the consequences and implications for their personal identities and for the future of Welsh nationhood of that ancient, hypnotic attraction. It also shows how Welsh self-perception and self-abasement are in part simply the deeply internalised converse of the condescending and sometimes dismissive way in which Wales tends to be viewed from the other, incomparably more privileged, side of the Severn Bridge. Thus when Glenys, 'Gonnie' Jones's early love who is now an innocent rookie nurse in London, accompanies him to a fashionable private viewing of a friend's art work, she is quickly made to feel unwelcome and uncomfortable by the response of other guests, who are reeking of affected good taste and studied sophistication. A young man slips a glass of white wine into her hand and strikes up an insinuating conversation that clearly requires from her an explanation of her anomalous presence:

'I came with Goronwy Jones,' Glenys said.

The young man's eyebrows raised to indicate a degree of rapid understanding.

'Oh,' he said, 'You're one of his, are you?'

'We come from the same place,' she said, 'in Wales. Our families are neighbours.'

The young man's eyes glazed over with evaporating interest.

'Oh, really,' he said.

His head swayed at the end of his long neck as he looked around for more worthwhile conversational pickings.

'I really must have a word with Archie,' he said. (J, 29)

Jones has long since equipped himself to cope with reactions such as this by virtually eliminating all telltale signs of his Welshness (such as his accent), developing what so many of those who get closest to knowing him call his self-protective 'carapace', and adopting an archness both of outlook and of expression which is evident when he has to endure two of his self-important and over-promoted colleagues busily ingratiating themselves with the College Principal:

> There was little point in screaming. His whole nature demanded an exit of such dignity that it would drive Blair and Jollikins like a pair of panting bullocks into the shade of his spreading magnanimity. But this was not easily done. These were protected specimens of an academic herd not easily stampeded and professionally unastonishable: wrapt in impenetrable increments of complacency and compound self-satisfaction. (J, 38)

Jones therefore repeatedly showcases Humphreys's satiric vision at its most sardonic. It also features deft switches of register, that become increasingly important as Jones's Welsh past encroaches ever more pressingly on his carefully policed self-protective present. The change is, for example, succinctly signalled when Jones, now back in the solitude of his own meagre bachelor flat, briefly exults in his victory over Jollikins only to collapse into ominous, morose self-dissatisfaction:

he was vouchsafed a clear vision of Jollikins's glistening features sagging under the gravitational pull of irreversible mortification. But Jones's cup was no longer capable of running over. His own face was sagging. With obsessive concern he fingered his cheeks and the loosening skin around his neck. (*J*, 39)

Jones is full of witty exposés of such creatures of the great metropolis as the predatory hedonist Wharton, who wags his finger at his Welsh friend while admonishing him to remember that 'Adolf believed in marriage as the final solution.' (*J*, 58) The London Welsh are also fastidiously skewered, as in the case of the velvet-collared MP of Jones's home constituency whom he meets outside a Welsh chapel in London and who 'occupied more space on the pavement than anyone else': his eyes, even as he is unctuously addressing his constituent, 'moved about, screening the members of the congregation as they passed by'. (*J*, 41) And then there is the galaxy of female sophisticates successively seduced by Jones's increasingly practised charms as a renowned 'ladies' man', many of whom also skilfully pander to his genuine and discriminating aesthetic tastes. Because Jones is sympathetically portrayed by Humphreys as a complex character part of whom really does blossom in a London context that, unlike the Wales he has known, can indeed nourish his highly developed, exquisitely cultured, sensibilities.

And that, of course, is the very nub of his insoluble difficulties. It is in part his attachment to London and identification with the self that the city has enabled him to become that inexorably distances him from a Glenys who is increasingly repelled by the city and drawn back to her Welsh roots and away from him. Yet his case is even more complex than that, because, as several of his most shrewd intimates point out, there is that in him that causes him to flee commitments and entanglements and responsibilities of any kind; that requires him ruthlessly to cultivate a self-sufficiency the sad face of which only becomes apparent when he stares in the mirror and is mercilessly confronted with his own remorselessly ageing fifty-seven-year-old features. By then he has realised that it was intuiting this that had eventually determined Glenys to break with him, not even to return to Wales but to emigrate to the USA as wife of a brilliantly-talented young neurosurgeon from Leicestershire. And paradoxically, as his onetime lover Annie shrewdly realises, it is this very self-containedness that has made him so devastatingly attractive to women, all of whom were deluded into thinking that they alone could break it down. He is a 'male Sleeping Beauty' they yearn to awaken with a kiss. (J, 120)

But Humphreys refuses to simplify this ruling trait of Jones's personality into mere selfishness. He skilfully allows for the sympathetic possibility that it is an involuntary reflex action, an instinctive recoil from any relationship or circumstance that threatens to 'imprison' him – in the way he had been imprisoned early in that dreadful pigsty and later, by a natural extension, by all that the pigsty had come to represent for him about the whole of rural Wales. No wonder that, as his bewildered mother remarks on her first visit to the strange foreign city of London, he has spent his life ever restlessly moving from flat to flat. It is she, too, who perceptively comments that he's become 'like a taxi-driver. Always close on the heels of fashion.' (J, 106) And it is his beloved mother's eventual passing that first and most deeply pierces Jones's carapace to briefly reveal an enduring, if fragile, attachment to his early background

Sympathy for poor Jones intensifies as, now in his later middle age and with physical decline already apparent, he bleakly comes to recognise the terrible price he has had to pay right down the London years to preserve his desperately cherished 'liberty'. But his self-defensive reaction unfortunately takes in part the form of a cruel, sadistic, demolition of the stubborn attachment to Wales of poor lost Idwal Davies, one of his last students, whose dumb appeals to his compatriot for moral support is met only with the sneering observation 'I'm not a professional exile.' (J, 100)

There are two complex signifiers that recur like leitmotifs in Wagnerian music throughout the novel, accumulating significance ever more rapidly as it draws to its conclusion. One of these is the Benin heads Jones has tastefully collected and that he sensuously caresses and adores partly because, as again Annie realises, they satisfy the 'natural born hoarder' in him, although she is unsure 'what great big inner trembling hereditary insecurity' it is that they protect him against. (*J*, 118) Those heads also serve as a synecdoche for the large collection of valuables he intends to present in his own memory to his College on his retirement, only to be shocked out of his intention by the realisation that there is enough animosity towards him on all sides abroad for the permanent safekeeping of that collection to be in jeopardy. He is therefore left alone, surrounded by precious accumulations that are no longer a defence but beginning to resemble the prison of his pathetic old age. And his failure to secure his legacy brings home to him the utter barrenness of his childless existence.

By the very end, his room, too, has turned from refuge into an untidy pigsty in which he is isolated and trapped just as he had been by his father at the very beginning of his life. The pigsty and the apple tree: the first of these twinned images from early memory thus reveals at the novel's conclusion the sad logic of its implications. As for the second, it signified from the very first the positive memories and experiences that, thanks to his mother, had also been laid down early in his life. The apple tree thus represented the potential that, sadly, he had refused to identify with and thus actualise.

He implicitly realises this when, after the doctor has told him that his mother had been 'felled' suddenly, he immediately makes the connection between her and the apple tree. Subsequently, he inserts the casket containing her mortal remains in the middle of the row of Benin heads on his mantelpiece, unconsciously thereby opening up the possibility that he might yet, however belatedly, opt for what she, rather than they, represented. And again when he becomes infatuated with the young Welsh activist Lowri, who for him is the spitting image of Glenys when young, he is actually so moved by what she represents of promise not only for the Welsh language but for his own elderly life that he images her and her cause as a tree in vigorous growth. But then again he can only revert to type and clumsily attempt to claim, and appropriate, her sexually as he had done all the women with whom he had casual relationships. So this last opportunity to redeem his life is lost, and Jones is left a sad, defeated, soul, mouldering in a small, cheerless flat.

Then, of course, there is that other dimension of significance that relates to the connection, already mentioned in this study, of the pig and the apple tree with the old story of Myrddin Wyllt, the wild man of the woods after the barbarous Battle of Arfderydd. Humphreys ends his poem about 'An Apple Tree and a Pig', part of the *Ancestor Worship* sequence, with Myrddin admitting that

> I have eaten the apple of knowledge and all I know
> Is that love must fail and lust must overthrow.
>
> And in the nights of winter when the ice-winds howl
> A pity and a terror fasten themselves upon my soul
>
> And I cry upon death to wrap his white redress
> Without mercy about the stillness of the merciless
> And remedy my madness with long silence. (*CP*, 81)

And even though Jones ends up a hermit very differently circumstanced from the legendary Myrddin Wyllt, he shares with him at the end of the novel a final condition of grim self-knowledge and despairing self-arraignment.

5

POEMS, ESSAYS, CULTURAL HISTORY

In 1999, when he had reached his eightieth birthday, Emyr Humphreys published his *Collected Poems*. Running to over 200 pages, this volume was a revelation for many who had come to know Humphreys only as a distinguished novelist. And as was the case with the fiction, these were clearly poems that had issued from the unsentimental heart of a moral intelligence. Of a cleansed and cleansing clarity, they brought to mind some lines from the poetry of the elegant American poet, Richard Wilbur: 'Seeing a bucket of perfectly lucid water / We fall to imagining prodigious honesties.'[1] And these works quietly accumulated over a period of more than half a century were, again like the novels, cerebral to the very marrow, because Humphreys strongly believes that we should always 'mind' what we do, and where we are.

Over the years, the poetry had acquired a kind of underground reputation, as samples appeared in various places, most notably in *Penguin Poets 27* (alongside the poetry of John Ormond and John Tripp), thanks to the initiative of the then-editor of the series, B. S. Johnson. Humphreys had met the experimental novelist while staying, on a University of Wales writing scholarship, at the university's attractive conference centre at Gregynog Hall, near Newtown. (It was there, too, that he was enabled to collaborate with the eminent Welsh composer Alun Hoddinott.) Such samples of his poetry as had occasionally appeared in print offered tantalising glimpses of its distinctive quality. The 1970 *Ancestor Worship* sequence in particular was rumoured to be a major achievement, although by 1999 copies of it had become virtually unobtainable. To reread that sequence in *The Collected Poems* was therefore to appreciate the way its stature grew from its power to reveal the full scale and consequence of Humphreys's lifelong preoccupations with country, language, power and art. With this came the realisation that his novels and poems were different aspects of a single complex whole. A symmetry therefore emerged: just as, at the very beginning, the first novel Humphreys ever wrote (and published in heavily revised form some fifteen years later as *A Toy Epic*) had grown directly out of his adolescent poetry, so, towards the latter end of his career, understanding of his poetry could be seen to grow best out of a familiarity with his novels. It could even be suggested, without the slightest prejudice as to their quality and significance, that his was a *novelist's* poetry. Its impulse was not introverted and lyrical, like most of the poetry of the day, but rather objectively distanced in character, featuring a fascination with other people's lives and circumstances. An early favourite of his was Browning's famous collection of poetic studies, aptly titled *Men and Women* (1855).

Humphreys had shown an interest in writing poems as well as stories from the very first. He had been introduced to *The New English Review*, and through it to the work of T. S. Eliot and Ezra Pound in particular, by his influential economics teacher Moses Jones while he was still a sixth former, and had then taken to ransacking the shelves of Rhyl library, a local 'Mecca' he credits with having been in effect a nursery of his talent. Pound's *Make It New* left an indelible mark on his mind, as did *The Cantos*, whose strange music haunted him even though he could make little sense of the contents. The poems of D. H. Lawrence attracted him more than the novels. He was intoxicated by the European reach of the learning of Pound and Eliot, and his exposure to the concentrated power of Imagist writing contributed to his development into a minimalist writer both of poetry and of prose. Some of the poems he wrote during this early period even found their way into print thanks to the support of Goronwy Rees, the Welshman who was then the literary editor of *The Spectator*.[2]

His interest in religious and metaphysical issues – he had, after all, at one point seriously considered becoming an Anglican priest – also found expression in his poetry, and the endless internal debate that was then begun, between faith in an ultimate purpose to life and a sceptical view of such fond illusions, has continued down to the present. He developed an admiration for Donne quite early, and then progressed, as he came to see it, to a measured appreciation of the more sober and succinct work of Herbert and of Vaughan. The opening stanza of his late poem 'Listening to Messiaen', for instance, shows him finding equivocal consolation in the harmonies and symmetries of music:

These are new devotions. The world to come
Glides and rustles among the trumpets
And the drums. The means and the measure. How else
Could you eavesdrop on the chatter of ghosts? Stringed
Promises can simplify our torments even
Overwhelm the percussive threats of retribution. (*CP*, 197)

Other late poems show him turning to the natural world (he became a dedicated walker in later years) for intimations of the mysterious underlying coherence of the universe:

Ultimate discoveries
Are made in winter
Snow on the bridge
And galaxies piercing the sky
Pinpricks in the velvet
Choreograph small lives
With giant steps, expose
Eyes in exile with distances
That defy calibration:
How far is far when it
Embraces near? (*CP*, 181)

Several of his poems have been 'occasional' poems, in that they arose from specific encounters and locations. It was a chance encounter with Joseph Losey at an arts festival Humphreys had organised at Llandeilo with his longtime patron Richard, Lord

Dinefwr, that prompted reflections on a director's unscrupulously cavalier treatment of 'stars':

> Clear the piazza! I want
> A marble chess-board to give her standing room
> The last piece left untaken
> Not quite naked but still
> A product anybody could eat. (*CP*, 68)

Being very much the product of their occasion, they can sometimes seem somewhat arcane and hermetic, as is the case with the sur-realistically strange little piece 'Rabbit Ensemble':

>   . . . I found
> A god-like rabbit nibbling my paper and
> In the one warm corner his long-eared consort
> Breaking my brittle pencil with the white tools
> Of her hostile teeth. (*CP*, 33)

It turns out to be a record of Humphreys's feelings on returning home to Britain from Italy at the end of the war and finding himself faced with the dilemma as to whether, as a newly-married man, he should knuckle under and become just another of life's 'rabbits' obediently nibbling away at their daily tasks or risk embarking on a career as a writer.

Some of his late poems are abstruse for a different reason: they are composed of a series of short sections, often deliberately un-punctuated and switching restlessly and unpredictably between Welsh and English, whose precise relationship to each other is difficult to determine. 'Inscribing Stones', for instances, opens with a reflection in Welsh arising directly from the experience of walking along a beach, only to segue into English in the next section to ponder more abstract question about eternal enigmas such as the nature of love and the relationship of life to eternity. The next few 'movements' begin with a reversion to Welsh in order to reflect on the role of the poet in a beleaguered culture, before shifting back to English to contrast the reactions of the Welsh and the Irish to such a dilemma. The concluding sections contemplate the traditional role of English education in Wales to prepare the people for admission to an English culture that nowadays offers them heroes from 'Ealing, Disneyland, and Slough'. And the tenth and final section is an elegiac musing on how long ago it all began and how it might end.

Humphreys's most notable poetic achievement, 'Ancestor Worship', is even more intricately composite in structure, consisting of seventeen poems that occupy twenty five pages of the *Collected Poems*. In many ways self-contained and free-standing they also constitute a loose single grouping of pieces roughly keyed to the theme of the relationship of present to past, and to related concerns such as the sometimes conflicting claims of different human allegiances, ranging from family, friends and acquaintances to society and its leaders. Recurrent throughout the sequence is the question of a how a writer chooses to position herself or himself in relation to these different claims, and in particular the vexed issue of the frequently ambivalent relationships creative writers have with power in both its benign and malign forms.

'A Roman Dream', completed during the Kennedy era when two immensely powerful modern Empires confronted each other in the Cuban crisis, takes the form of a writer's frenzied attempts in ancient Rome to escape the clutches of the soldiers sent by the demented Emperor (Nero? Caligula?) to arrest him and hold him to Imperial account. A portrait of the writer as (reluctant) conscientious objector, 'A Roman Dream' contrasts suggestively with another poem in the sequence, 'Poet of the Old North', that confronts the fact that the earliest Welsh poets were obedient servants and celebrators of the warlords of their period. This sobering reminder is partially offset by recollection of the ancient Welsh legend about Myrddin Wyllt. Yet even the traumatised Myrddin has darkly to concede in Humphreys's poem that 'All men wait for battle and when it comes / Pass along the sword's edge their resilient thumb.' (*CP*, 80)

In some of the poems, the poet contrives his own Myrddin-like retreat in memory to the loving company of relatives, most particularly

107

his father and the beloved father-in-law who lived with Humphreys's family for sixteen years. Something of the ambivalent innocence of such a figure (also wonderfully captured in the character of J.T. in *Outside the House of Baal*) is captured in 'Twenty-Four Pairs of Socks' by means of an affectionate recollection of how in his helpless impracticality the ageing minister had, in fact, come to rely on the compliant ministrations of others. But particularly memorable is Humphreys's great tribute, in the opening poem 'Ancestor Worship', to his Welsh poetic ancestors who played such a vital role in the very creation during the immediate post-Roman era of a people and a language that their poems had continued to sustain in being ever since:

> They were all poets
> They all wove
> Syllabic love into their wooden homes
>
> They saw the first invaders come
> Pushing their boats through the water meadows
> Their teeth and their swords glittering in the stealthy light
> And they carved metrical systems out of their own flesh.
>   * * *
> The air is still committed to their speech
> Their voices live in the air
> Like leaves like clouds like rain
> Their words call out to be spoken
> Until the language dies
> Until the ocean changes. (*CP*, 75)

The poems in *Collected Poems* were grouped by the author into eight sections which, he explained, have a degree of autobiographical intent. That linking of 'autobiography' with intent is, as has already been seen in this study, a lifelong characteristic of a writer who, from the outset, had felt a very strong moral obligation to *choose* how to live, and who insisted on recognising the social implications and the social consequences of the choices available.

After all, as has already been noted, the very first poem he published was 'A Young Man Considers his Possibilities', a title Humphreys has recalled as constituting a kind of homage to W. B. Yeats, who was fond of such formulations. Yet, of course, war descended on Humphreys willy-nilly, and among his other early poems are 'war poems' of an unorthodox kind: 'A Landscape in Hyde Park' explores the incongruous but convenient way in which 'blitz' could rhyme with 'bliss' in a young lover's experience, and 'Eddie' considers how 'mechanised war' could be the unlikely means of liberating a young lad from working-class drudgery. For a conscientious objector (such as Humphreys became) to recognise as much involved a magnanimous act of empathy, the telltale sign perhaps of the novelist already being incubated by the poetry.

War, however, brought Humphreys to the sharpest of choices: whether to fight or not to fight. The emotionally charged moral issues involved are explored in 'Courage' ('Swing the emotion to the heroic pitch / Then whip the fleshy horse over the deadly ditch' (*CP*, 7)) and 'Cowardice' ('I am the field of war, where good and bad / Mingle and batter and break' (*CP*, 7)). Crucial to the resolving of them – and later central to Humphreys's whole life and work – was his countercultural respect for religious dissent. This is explored in 'A Nonconformist', a poem that imagines:

> Jesus quietly pointing at my courage:
> 'Follow me in the face of hostile crowds
> Weapons derision hatred scorn . . . ' (*CP*, 5)

He also admired nonconformity in the more general, secular applications of the term. Hence in part his later fascination with the emotional risks taken by performers ('Actors X and Y'). Keeping company during the 1950s with such theatrical talents as Richard Burton, Peter O'Toole and Siân Phillips, Humphreys came to appreciate that, although they exposed themselves in ways that were very different from that of the poor vulnerable flasher 'Hugo', actors still shared with such the risk of seeming pathetically absurd.

As 'Director with Star' (where the speaker declares 'my cash machine will transform / Her smile into cash' (*CP*, 68)) and 'Show Business' (*CP*, 165–6) both indicate, the worlds of drama and film also furnished Humphreys with examples of the impulse to dominate and control, which he felt was a sinister constant in human affairs. Alarmed in the 1960s by what Herman Melville graphically called the 'power unanointed' of the USA ('Thing is when you exercise power / You put bits of the planet like Indians / In Reservations for their own good'), he caught the crude essence of such a mentality as we have seen in 'A Roman Dream':

> Last night the Emperor painted his face green,
> We all agreed this was the correct colour.
> I was a little drunk. I agreed too much. (*CP*, 78)

However, Humphreys was aware that such a luridly monstrous example of megalomania, further suggesting the evil shades of Hitler, did not truly represent the form that power most dangerously took in the post-war world. Viewed from the perspective of the 'postcolonial' thinking of his master, Saunders Lewis, Humphreys's Wales was threatened most by the hegemonic power of Anglo-American capitalism, mediated most insidiously through the mass media (and related means of institutionalised control) of a heavily centralised and anglocentric state. In such poems as 'Bullocks' and 'Turkeys in Wales', Humphreys created his own Orwellian parables of the resulting state of conformity:

> Certain turkeys survive
> They believe in their exemption
> Attribute
> Their extra days
> To the music
> Of their eloquence
> And their influence
> With the Owners. (*CP*, 66)

How a writer relates to the politics of power has always been a deep concern of one who has been a conscientious objector, a pacific nationalist, and a Welsh-language activist. A beautiful early poem contemplates with gentle, sympathetic irony Virgil's pastoral retreat from confronting contemporary atrocities and abuses: 'One would hardly consider Vergil lacking in feeling: / It was just that news from the East travelled so slow.' (*CP*, 18) Humphreys has however always known that retreat is not really an option – a political message being always secreted in the very medium an artist uses. Working in TV made him aware there was no such thing as an innocent image, all is manipulation, and in 'The Duchess and her Duke' (based on the Duke and Duchess of Windsor) he shows how the massage is the message: 'The day the photograph was taken / The congregation of tulips in the open bowl / Were well-bred and fleshy'. (*CP*, 43)

Landscapes, his second major sequence, consisting in this case of a set of short poems intended to be set to music by Alun Hoddinott, could have been entitled 'past-scapes'. It is a powerful demonstration of the difference that, in a colonised Wales, what we don't know makes to what we see. Locations rich with the facts, legends, actions and experiences of human history become reduced to mere topography once the past has been allowed to escape, a people's memory lost (and won, or won over, by new allegiances). Because, as he writes in 'Betws Garmon', 'When places love people / Mountains are messages / Stone words against the sky.' (*CP*, 103) How to restore a nation's ability to read those messages, those stone words, has always been the dilemma that has proved for him the most potent source of creativity, and in *Ancestor Worship* the sequence form allows him the freedom to create as sharply multifaceted an image of the conundrum as may be found in Cubist painting.

But of course the novel form also provides an obvious model for this novelist's poetry. An elderly woman become forgetful ('I'm a silly old woman. Forget my own name next' (*CP*, 91)); a farm transmogrified into a modern estate; an old minister and his mummified sermons (*CP*, 99); through characters and incidents such as these does the sequence plot its course, so that in total it comes to seem a touchingly domestic *memento mori* of an ailing culture. And, as always, it is to Welsh writing that Humphreys looks to ensure the transmission of a culture in defiance of all that is seemingly empowered by History itself to effect its demise. Indeed, traces may be found in his own poetry of the style of the war poems of the ancient seventh-century poet of the 'Old North', Taliesin,[3] bard to the great war leader Urien and one of the founding fathers of the Welsh strict metre tradition: 'Unreproducible blunt rhymes / Like the breath in his lungs / Made short and immediate by danger.' (*CP*, 76)

Indeed, Humphreys is anxious to ensure that the ghosts of the great Welsh-language writers 'move easily between [his own English] words':

> The dead are horizontal and motionless
> They take less room
> Than the stones which mark the tomb
>
> But the words they spoke
> Grow like flowers in the cracked rock
>
> Their ghosts move easily between words
> As people move between trees
> Gathering days and sunlight
> Like fuel for an invisible fire. (*CP*, 75)

The enabling strategies developed for this purpose in *Collected Poems* include the scattering throughout the text of translations from the Welsh, and the insertion, in the latter part of the book, of a body of Welsh-language poetry written by Humphreys himself. This is largely the outcome of the period, late in his career, when he was regularly scripting plays and films for S4C. In turn, it highlights the fact that this *Collected Poems* was very largely the record of Humphreys's rebirth as a poet; over the dozen or so years immediately preceding its publication, he had revised much of his early work and added to it new poetry amounting to about a third of the collection in all.

One feature of Humphreys's work, however, has remained constant over the sixty or years of his career, namely the fact that his poetry is wholly unlike any other poetry that has been written in modern Wales; and in this difference lies its significance – its power to make a difference to the way in which people (and most particularly his own people, the Welsh) think of themselves and their world. Richard Wilbur likened the ordinary movements of the human mind to those of a bat treating the limits of its familiar habitat as already and inalterably given, and thus able 'darkly [to know] what obstacles are there'. But then Wilbur reveals that flaw, that chink, in the simile that lets in a poetry, such as that of Emyr Humphreys, that can let out and liberate the mind, not only of a 'subaltern' individual but of a colonised nation: 'The mind is like a bat. Precisely. Save / That in the very happiest intellection / A graceful error may correct the cave.'[4]

* * *

In 2002 Emyr Humphreys published *Conversations and Reflections*, a collection of thirteen of the essays he had published over the previous half century, interspersed with four lengthy interviews. The suggestion for such a volume had come from Richard, Lord Dinefwr, who had much regretted his inability to read the conversations with Humphreys through the medium of Welsh that had recently appeared under the title *Dal Pen Rheswm* (1999). Richard Dinefwr was a generous, longstanding patron of Humphreys. It was thanks to his financial support that Humphreys had been enabled to make a film version of R. S. Thomas's poem 'The Airy Tomb' in the 1950s and the original edition of the seminal study of Welsh social, cultural and political history *The Taliesin Tradition* was originally published in 1983 under the auspices of Dinefwr's Black Raven Press.

As for *Conversations and Reflections* it stands as an indispensable introduction to the extensive intellectual hinterland of Humphreys's creative work. Its contents are imaginatively arranged so as to reflect the subtle interconnectedness of the writer's reflections on his life, his work, the work of others, the politics of culture and the culture of politics. Humphreys grew to manhood during the 1930s, an Age of Anxious Uncertainties and Dogmatically Certain Isms. Much of the material in this volume shows him working out a viable view of his contemporary world and a reading of its past that would accommodate both his sense of vocation and his sense of responsibility to the Welsh collective.

In being addressed to matters that were particular pressing concerns at the time when they were written, many of the essays stand as a valuable record of twentieth-century Welsh cultural history and accordingly convey the tension and drama of their occasion. No closeted writer, Humphreys had engaged throughout the period of his maturity in political activism on behalf of the Welsh language even while producing a remarkable body of creative work – poems, historical overviews, literary criticism, plays (for radio and television) and of course an entire world of fiction. But the elegant trenchancy of the writing endows his 'occasional' essays with the power to long outlive the several different circumstances that originally called them into being.

The material is impressive in its breadth of vision, as Humphreys's intelligence ranges far and wide, from sixth-century Wales to later twentieth-century 'media studies' (his is a shrewd portrait of the BBC Monitor mogul, Sir Huw Wheldon, scion of a Welsh Calvinistic dynasty). There is always a sharp political edge to his discussion of Welsh cultural issues, and his analysis of the ideology underpinning Matthew Arnold's passion for the 'Celtic' is a small masterpiece of 'post-colonial criticism'.

In many ways, Humphreys may be thought of as a writer-intellectual in the Continental tradition (think of Václav Havel) – one who believes it is a writer's duty to bring creative intelligence to bear on any issue that concerns the preservation of civilised social order. The social order that has specifically concerned him throughout his long, distinguished career is, of course, that of Wales, and *Conversations and Reflections* represents an important extension of what he has memorably called 'The Taliesin Tradition', the spinal contribution made by writers (particularly poets) from the sixth century onwards to the preservation and transmission of a distinctively Welsh cultural identity. This, Humphreys has written, 'has contrived to be a major factor in the . . . fragile concept of Welsh nationhood, which has persisted stubbornly down to the present day . . . without the exercise of military or political power and without any indigenous control of the economic base'. (*TT*, 2–3)

In addition to being valuable cultural documents, the essays are also illuminating of their author's creative work, whether they address the various cultural commitments from which his writing derives its force and takes its bearings ('The Third Difficulty'), the vexed issue of readership ('The Empty Space'), or details of genre and technique ('Notes on the Novel'). What is on offer is a map of the historical and cultural background of his powerful creative publications, and the complementary conversations add further detail to that map by exploring some of the intellectual concerns and motifs that have regularly recurred throughout all his published output.

But there is also an intriguing sense in which several of these essays are miniature narratives or character sketches, unexpected instances of a novelist's art. Each group of essays is roughly keyed to the conversation that precedes it. Echoes of Emyr Humphreys's comments on the significance of place and time in the first conversation are to be heard in the essays that follow; the political and cultural values to which the lives and actions, as well as the writings, of authors may bear witness is a theme of the second conversation duly amplified in the next group of essays that includes a classic imaginative portrait of his intellectual master, Saunders Lewis; 'A Lost Leader' and 'Television and Us' include reflections on modern mass media, an aspect of the process of globalisation that is of pressing and intimate concern to Emyr Humphreys in the third conversation; and as the discussion of the late novella *Ghosts and Strangers* (2001) leads the novelist on, in the fourth conversation, to consider wider issues of fictional form, so does the final group of essays bring together his writings about the forms that fiction might take in present culture and underline the inflexible respect for the unique genius of a language that is the hallmark of the 'born' writer.

But the interrelationships between the different elements of *Conversations and Reflections* are not as one-dimensional as the foregoing would suggest, nor is the flow of thought in one direction only. Writings anticipate discussions to come as well as echoing those that have gone, illuminating remarks in conversations radiate meaning backwards as well as forwards, and juxtaposed essays strike up an interesting conversation with each other. The overall impression is of a creative intelligence whose constant integrity of purpose nevertheless allows of sallies of daring thought in new, unexpected directions at the promptings of an irrepressible intellectual curiosity.

In his dazzlingly resourceful essay 'The Crucible of Myth', Emyr Humphreys shows how symbol, legend and myth can provide privileged deep access to the formative underlying constants of Welsh history and the Welsh psyche. The famous Celtic cauldron of rebirth, for instance, is shown to have functioned as a seminal image for a people (stateless to this day) whose very survival has depended on constant, stubborn self-reinvention. And the many successive transformations integral to that endlessly adaptive process are captured in the story of the little servant Gwion bach, from the *Mabinogion* tales, who becomes the great shape-changing wizard Taliesin after accidentally swallowing three drops of magical brew for the magical transformation of her son being stirred in a cauldron by the witch Ceridwen.

But this native strain of mythology, supremely manifest in the *Mabinogion*, is then adversely contrasted in the companion essay 'Taliesin's Children' with that foreign strain of 'British' fantasy, centred on the English appropriation of the Welsh Arthur as national hero, that began increasingly to occupy the Welsh mind and thus insidiously direct the course of Welsh history. And it is this anglicisation of the Welsh imagination that Humphreys sees in his brilliant, incisive and dryly amusing essay 'Arnold in Wonderland' as being finally fatally reinforced in the middle of the nineteenth century by Matthew Arnold's seemingly judicious and authoritative lectures conveniently contrasting the primitive, regressive charm of the dreamy, melancholy, poetical and impractical Celts with the world domination of the practical, progressive English. As Humphrey pithily puts it, for Arnold 'C of E' stood for the Culture of England.

Essays such as these are intoxicating in their sweeping visionary conspectus of Welsh history. Very different is that set of essays that succinctly address the novelist's art. 'The Third Difficulty', for instance, asks how a form of storytelling perfectly adapted to the needs of nineteenth-century bourgeois society can possibly survive in the post-bourgeois era of modern media and com- munications. In the resulting discussion Humphreys generously acknowledges the remarkable potential of these new technologies. He emphasises that present-day novelists must recognise the radical change of consciousness effected by the new media and rethink their own narrative techniques in consequence. But he also argues that the essential, continuing value of the contemporary novel, 'cottage industry' though it may have become, resides in the power it inherently retains as a traditional form to counterbalance, and even partially to counteract, the commodification and ersatz multi- nationalism of a globalised capitalist media industry. 'One of the aims of the realist novel in the age of the mass media', he writes, 'should be to initiate a chain reaction of readership that will in some measure, however small, subvert the stultifying power of communications technology.' (CR, 208)

Furthermore, as he goes on to emphasise in 'The Empty Space', this service that the novel alone can offer is of particular, vital, importance in the case of a small people like the Welsh: after all, their very future depends on preserving that special relationship with their own, specific, human and natural environment that allows them to maintain a living connection with their unique cultural tradition. It is in this context that Humphreys repeatedly proclaims all his novels to have been the work of a devoted 'People's Remembrancer'. To which, in 'Notes on the Novel', he adds the adage: 'the main function of the novelist remains to celebrate; and by one means or another to perpetuate the language of the tribe.' (*CR*, 227)

Several of Humphreys's essays take spectacular advantage of his gifts as storyteller and for sharply delineating character. This is how his memorable portrait of Saunders Lewis begins, 'A narrow white face above a large steering wheel. Recognizable even in a squat car hurtling down an Aberystwyth street. There is a schoolgirl in the back enjoying the ride. And there he is. The necessary figure.' (*CR*, 84) A long essay ('The Night of the Fire') about the Penyberth incident that had been the baptism of fire of his own adolescent imagination, brings out the theatrical nature of the occasion and the trial that followed: 'the ventilation was bad. The High Sheriff, Mr Ronald Armstrong Jones, father of the distinguished photographer, could be seen leaning back in his chair, stifling yawns and staring fixedly at the ceiling.' (*CR*, 114) The casual insolence of colonial mastery could scarcely have been more economically captured. The same technique is employed even when very different subjects are addressed. 'Perhaps the solitary genius of the cinema to emerge in England was a little fat boy from the grey London suburb of Leytonstone. It hardly needs extensive Freudian analysis to trace the fantasies of a fat boy who never grew up in the technically perfect cinematography of Alfred Hitchcock.' (*CR*, 204) And on occasion Humphreys can also draw on memories of his own personal encounters with prominent individuals to deliver the *coup de gras* of a devastating *bon mot*:

> I am not sure that Huw [Wheldon] ever understood that there is more to culture than taking tea with the Queen Mother. At times he seemed mesmerised by the sound of Sir Kenneth Clark dispensing critical aperçus about the work of often penniless and suicidal artists through (if I may coin an anatomical surrealism) his well-heeled nose. (*CR*, 148)

The cutting edge of Humphreys's writing is, however, never more apparent than when engaging with some of the most pressing cultural threats of the day to Wales and the Welsh language. In

'Television and Us' he wrote an insider's exposé of a medium and an industry whose inherent English bias posed, from the very beginning, a huge threat to whatever remained of independent Welsh thought. It was an essay published when the demand, supported by Humphreys, for a separate Welsh-language television channel was really beginning to pick up steam. As a former, and highly experienced, TV professional himself, he well knew that the impression given by the medium that it was nothing but a neutral 'window on the world' was completely false. It was, he insisted, inherently a medium of illusion, fantasy and ideology. And as the Russian film industry had realised as early as the 1920s, it was an ideal instrument for indoctrination and propaganda. But what in Soviet hands was used to promote a socialist, proletarian revolutionary society, was in England used instead to reinforce the world-outlook of the powerfully entrenched English middle classes. And of course right across Western society, television became the instrument of an increasingly powerful capitalist and consumerist culture.

From all such insights as this it followed that for Wales to survive it had to gain control over its own means of television production if it was not to remain wholly in thrall to an anglocentric medium. The essay then traces the long history of the struggle, from the 1930s onwards, to establish a radio and television system in Wales with at least a modicum of self-control, although Humphreys pessimistically concludes that in reality very little has changed even though both the BBC and the Independent companies now (in 1974) cannily flaunt a very superficial 'Welsh' identity. But he ends his essay by hoping that the Welsh may yet choose to mobilise what remains of their cultural memory to ensure this powerfully influential modern medium is used to creative and beneficial ends, by celebrating and advancing their own existence.

As, then, this last essay again confirms, *Conversations and Reflections* is something very much more than a loose collection of interviews and occasional pieces. It is an integrated work that is a major cultural document and it is likely to prove one of Emyr Humphreys's most enduring achievements as a writer.

* * *

Towards the end of 'Television and Us', Humphreys proposes a simplified, but highly suggestive, model of the Welsh past that, he acidly remarks, might 'at least have the merit of relating the marmoreal shapes of academic history to the continuing problem of human behaviour'. (*CR*, 179) A similar intention could be said to underlie *The Taliesin Tradition*, a remarkable book-length overview of Welsh history that, like 'The Crucible of Myth', is based on the (unhistoric) assumption that the state of a people's psyche is symbolically recorded in myths and legends that are then translated into those actions, events and experiences that we have learned to call 'history'. Another notable contemporary example of such an approach is *Survival* by Margaret Atwood, a Canadian writer highly conscious of the permanent looming presence of the neighbouring USA. *The Taliesin Tradition* is then what might be termed a 'psychography', and as such it belongs to a tradition of mythic histories of the Welsh that includes Morgan Llwyd's seventeenth-century work *Llyfr y Tri Aderyn*, Charles Edwards's *Y Ffydd Ddi-Ffuant* from the same century, and Theophilus Evans's eighteenth-century *Drych y Prif Oesoedd*, all religious classics dismissively labelled 'pseudo-histories' by mainstream historians. But the myth of history advanced by *The Taliesin Tradition* has also functioned as an enabling 'supreme fiction' for Humphreys the novel writer, a master narrative that provides him with what the story of Ulysses provided for James Joyce and *The Golden Bough* for Eliot: a means of organising and making sense of the amorphousness of quotidian (Welsh) experience.

The Taliesin Tradition is moreover proof that, as Lucas Parry remarked in the *Land of the Living* sequence, the Welsh are a 'pattern-making people', a remark the truth of which Humphreys has affirmed in his essay on 'The Empty Space – Creating a Novel'. (*CR*, 211) In that essay he elaborates further on this core conviction:

There are sound historical reasons for this pattern-making habit. A small nation living for so many centuries under a state of siege – whether military, economic or cultural – needs defence in depth. There seems to me to be an intimate relationship between the ditches and ramparts of the Iron Age Celts and the stylised injunctions and commandments of the Methodists' *Cyffes Ffydd* and *Rhodd Mam*. (CR, 211)

To this he adds a revealing personal confession: 'in the case of *one* Welsh novelist, pattern-making is a life-long habit'. And nowhere has that facility of his been made more stimulatingly evident than in *The Taliesin Tradition*.

The riddle that Humphreys sets out to solve in *The Taliesin Tradition* is the mysterious survival of a people (the Welsh) that by rights should have disappeared very shortly after the Normans invaded these shores a millennium ago. And his solution? It is to argue that the Welsh have owed their survival down to the present day to what he terms 'the Taliesinic Tradition'. By this he means two things. First, the poetic and cultural legacy of the seventh-century poet Taliesin who was one of the founders of the great tradition of strict-metre poetry unique to the Welsh language and who, as himself a poet serving a beleaguered tribal minority, established the role of the 'bard' to be that of celebrant and custodian of his people's culture. And second, that need for repeated, eternally vigilant, cultural adaptation and self-invention in the face of chronic threat that was drummed into the Welsh people from their very beginning by their powerful myth of that other Taliesin, the wizard and great indefatigable shape-shifter.[5]

With an ingenuity and resourcefulness matching that of the great Taliesin himself, Humphreys then proceeds to demonstrate how all the leading events and characters of Welsh history may be seen as conforming to this root strategy of survival embodied in the figure of the legendary wizard figure. In the process he shows how very precarious and ambivalent a strategy it is, since adaptation can so easily become the prelude to complete assimilation. Indeed, in the latter pages of his study he argues that it is sadly this latter aspect of shape-shifting that has been the bane of Welsh history over the last couple of centuries. By way of evidence he points to the way in which the nineteenth-century Nonconformist Wales of the chapels and the Liberal party consisted of an attempt by the Welsh, following the notorious mid-century attack by English commissioners on their language and culture in the Blue Books Report of 1847 on the state of education, to adapt obediently to the demands of the modern age. This resulted only in the wholesale cowing and radical depoliticisation of a people desperately intent only on gaining respect and success by emulating the values and *mores* of bourgeois England. The same process so destructive of national identity was then repeated during the twentieth century, but this time with the heavily centralist Welsh Labour movement intent only on capturing the heights of the English economic, social and political systems. And as this study has already emphasised, Humphreys saw in these modern examples only an action replay of Welsh behaviour over the crucial decades immediately following the installation of the supposedly Welsh Tudor dynasty on the English throne.

The application of this thesis to the whole of Welsh history from the earliest Christian centuries to the present results in readings that are dazzlingly original and correspondingly incessantly controversial. In the process Humphreys exhibits a prodigal inventiveness. Central to the whole exercise is the conviction that ever since their emergence as a Romano-Celtic formation after the withdrawal of the legions, the Welsh people have only ever survived through resistance, and that the Taliesin Tradition has down the millennia proved the most effective way of maintaining such a resistance. While never intending either to slight or to overlook the materialist determinants of history rightly emphasised by professional historians, Humphreys contrastingly chooses to highlight the influence of mindset on the outcome of events.

Accordingly, he foregrounds the struggle for the Welsh mind between the wondrous, spellbinding tales of Arthur spun by the Anglo-Norman 'proto-novelist' Geoffrey of Monmouth, the supreme four-square propagandist of the future English Empire, and the magical indigenous productions of the modestly anonymous author of the restlessly shape-shifting stories of the *Mabinogion*.[6] He sees this struggle and its decisive outcome in favour of Arthur as decisively setting the tone and direction of Welsh history thereafter. As a modern novelist of the Welsh, Humphreys implicitly situates himself as humble heir to the genius of the *Mabinogion*. And indeed, when he launches into his own enchanting paraphrase of the stories, it is almost as if the personality of the twentieth-century author merges with or even, Taliesin-like, morphs into that of the medieval storyteller.

Humphreys proceeds to employ this thesis to illuminate the high road to London trodden by the Welsh carpetbaggers of Tudor and Elizabethan times; the seminal role of John Dee,[7] the London-Welsh Merlin, in planting in Elizabeth's head the notion that the Welsh 'discovery' of North America ahead of Columbus made that continent the legitimate possession of her England; the reconnection with the bardic past enabled by the eccentric but invaluable salvage acts of 'perpetual clergy' like Ieuan Brydydd Hir, the irascible and permanently impecunious curate; and the late eighteenth-century reinvention of Welsh identity by the Methodist genius William Williams Pantycelyn. He naturally makes much of that most Taliesinic of figures, Iolo Morganwg, the greatest and most eccentric creative mythographer of the modern Welsh, whose fascination with Madoc's 'discovery' of America led to John Evans's epic 2,000 mile journey in 1797 to the headwaters of the Missouri in order to visit Madoc's 'descendants', the Mandans. But the most startling applications of his model of Welsh history become apparent only when he deals with figures and events of recent centuries.[8]

Iolo named his son Taliesin, but more colourfully Taliesinic were Ab Ithel and Myfyr Morganwg, both of whom believed that 'Christianity was no more than druidism dressed in Jewish gaberdine'. (*TT*, 142) Even more luridly bizarre was William Price, often to be seen dressed in a green robe edged with scarlet and with a fox-skin cap on head, who, in good Unitarian fashion, named his son Iesu Grist.[9] This fusion of Unitarianism with Druidism found its apogee in the work of the great American architect Frank Lloyd Wright, grandson of a Cardiganshire Unitarian, who in due course explained how he had come by the name of two of his greatest houses: 'I chose a Welsh name . . . and it was Taliesin. Taliesin, a druid, was a member of King Arthur's Round Table.' (*TT*, 161) As for Lloyd George, although clearly a Taliesin figure by background, inclination and early political career, and accordingly endowed with irresistible poetic eloquence, he went on to become a renegade Merlin, or even perhaps 'an Arthurian Messiah'. (*TT*, 192) Yet for final resting place he chose not Westminster Abbey but a wonderfully romantic spot on the banks of the Dwyfor near his home village of Llanystumdwy. It was, however, the staunchly pro-British Arthurian strain in post-Galfridian Welsh history that continued inexorably to prevail, and Humphreys makes ingenious play with the influence of the likes of Arthur Gould (great rugby international) on the popular Welsh psyche and of heroic miners' leaders such as Arthur Cooke and Arthur Horner on twentieth-century Welsh social and political history.

The Taliesin Tradition is to modern Welsh literary culture what William Carlos Williams's remarkable book *In the American Grain* (1925) is to the literary culture of the USA: a groundbreaking study of poetic intensity, epic scope and profound consequence. It is a visionary work with a prophetic core. It is a modern jeremiad, a rebuke and a warning to the Welsh people that if they continue to stray from the path laid down by Taliesin, if they ignore or abuse his legacy, then the nation will inevitably perish. There is therefore about his work more than a hint of *The Ruin of Britain* ('*De Excidio Brittanniae*'), by the eighth-century monk Gildas. A diatribe to which Humphreys several times alludes, it 'addressed the secular and religious leadership of the British people as if . . . they had fallen from the grace which had gone with the amplitude of Romano-Christian civilization'. (*TT*, 8) And this, of course, is the subliminal message carried by much of his fiction, the greatest of his novels prominently included.

6

FICTION: LAST PHASE

The air of mellow reflection radiated by *Collected Poems* and *Conversations and Reflections* is thoroughly misleading. Throughout his seventies and on well into his eighties Humphreys remained almost as productive and as creatively vigorous as he had been in his youth and prime. In addition to the two titles mentioned, and the concluding novel in *The Land of the Living* sequence, his output during this period included three further novels and two short story collections. Then in his ninetieth year he published yet another collection of stories. And several of these later works found him revisiting and reinvigorating his longstanding interest in the Continental European context of Welsh experience.

In the case of *Unconditional Surrender* it could scarcely have been otherwise, as the novel is set in the immediate aftermath of Victory in Europe, and the terrible consequent problem of what to do with the past is explored partly through the plight of Cecilia von Leiden, a German 'countess' conveniently 'elderly' at fifty-seven. Complete with purloined family jewels, she has found 'refuge' (as she euphemistically puts it) in Wales, but now restive fellow-residents of the Residential Home For Decayed Gentlewomen in which she has been settled are maliciously campaigning for her repatriation. Hers is one of the two voices to be heard in the novel, the other being that of a Rector, middle-aged son of a hill farmer, who has himself taken 'refuge' in the Church of England. A gentle man of timid, fearful temperament, Edward Pritchard is troubled in conscience by the countess's plight while also increasingly unsettled by the conduct of his feisty young teenage daughter, Meg, and his beloved wife of twenty-seven years, the ever-faithful Olwen, who is incubating an infatuation with Colonel Bacon, the confident, briskly English military officer who is in charge of the local Prisoner of War camp.

In one sense, the whole novel is a structure of triadic relation-ships that allow Humphreys to explore issues some of which he himself could well have been alive to fifty years earlier. There is the intense, gendered, conspiratorial relationship between the three women – the Countess, Meg and her mother – who in some respects define themselves against the Rector. There is the guilty emotional scheming in which the Countess indulges in an attempt to under-mine the close, if increasingly troubled, family relationship of husband, wife and daughter. Intergenerational conflict, rend-ered instantly acute at a historical juncture when the future of the whole world seems at stake, is enacted through the tense triangular relationship between Meg and her suitor, Griff, heated idealists both, and the Rector, who has spent his life cultivating a worldly pragmatism that will protect him from the pain of moral challenge. Then there is the love-triangle at the apex of which is Meg, who finds her emotions divided (very much like those of the young Amy Parry of the *Land of the Living* sequence) between the innocent young Welsh farm-hand Griff, an ardent Welsh nationalist, and Klaus, a young German prisoner of war of great delicacy of sens-ibility; a confirmed internationalist and sly womaniser-in-waiting, he is a gifted musician and holds a strong sensual as well as intel-lectual attraction for one on the very brink of full womanhood. One is reminded that immediately after the war, Humphreys him-self had briefly hesitated between returning to Wales and turning European by settling in Italy.

And one is reminded also that one of Humphreys's deepest central concerns throughout his career has been how, and how far, the Welsh past should be allowed to influence the Welsh present. This issue, already explored as we have seen in *A Man's Estate*, is explored again with like complexity and in a similarly sombre key in *Unconditional Surrender*. Like all the English, the text implies, Colonel Bacon is really concerned not with the post-war re-construction of a devastated Europe but with the recovery of the

British Empire. But the Countess harbours no illusions: 'The Americans will throw a cloud of nauseating uniformity all over it, your British Empire. What's left of your world they will turn into commercial colonies and playgrounds. All noise and basic English. Quite horrid.' (*US*, 75) Many of the characters in the novel, Klaus prominently included, are desperately anxious that a murderous age of aggressive nationalisms should be conclusively over, and that no irritating and destabilising petty nationalisms should be allowed to sprout up anew in tiny little countries like Wales.

As for the Countess, she is torn in her attitude to the war and its prelude. On the one hand, the subterfuges she has been so skilfully practising and the lies and half-truths in which she has liberally indulged mean that she lives in constant terror of any revelation of the complex truth about her German background – that includes a family history of fellow-travelling with the Nazi party. On the other hand, she cannot bring herself to relinquish her 'right' to the estates of her late husband and to such wealth as they represented. The family jewels, the pride and joy of her old age, are treasure she can use to influence people, even to buy their 'affection', but they are also a tangible link with her personal past and guarantor, in her eyes, of her continuing right to inherited privileges she cannot bring herself to relinquish. Yet her claim to them is extremely dubious. She had been persuaded by her then second husband, a rackety Anglo-Irishman who worked in the film industry, to 'abscond with the family silver' (*US*, 80), to the outrage of relatives who are now intent on reclaiming it.

Given to occasionally voicing a nostalgia, like that of her late 'oma' ('grandmother'), for the Austro-Hungarian Empire, the Countess is actually unwilling to disavow her German identity, arguing disingenuously and yet truthfully that Bach, Schubert and Goethe had nothing to do with Nazism. Hers is therefore a cultural nationalism that actually chimes with that of Meg and Griff, although she refuses to recognise it, and even the rabidly anti-nationalist Klaus, who angrily renounces his own German allegiances, actually trades implicitly on his cultural legacy when he opts to beguile listeners by playing the incomparable music of the greatest German composers.

The Rector prefers his past to be safely dead and buried – he devotes himself to lovingly restoring an ancient memorial stone and to meticulously recording the history of his inconsequential little parish. By contrast, a 'small plump Baptist minister' (*US*, 63) at the political hustings blathers on about the three 'p's that have been the glory of Welsh life: 'the princes for freedom and independence – the poets for celebration of a better life, – the preachers to bring us vision and give us moral fibre.' (*US*, 63) As for Meg and Griff, both harbour a utopian dream of a Wales that chooses to access and mobilise its past in order to participate in the building of an exciting new post-war world order. This will see the tired old giant nation states that have caused all the carnage replaced by small political units dedicated to respecting and serving the needs of all their constituent members.

But then, all the main characters are also clearly revealed to be in personality and outlook the sum total of their own inescapable private, personal pasts. Meg and her mother both are idealists partly by virtue of a Nonconformist upbringing that had helped determine the values by which they live. The ostensibly unscrupulous and endlessly scheming Countess was a plain, unloved child, bossed by her nannies and tutors, who therefore had to learn early all the cunning arts of survival. Her condition was exacerbated by an unhappy marriage to a Graf who turned out to be a closet gay and a subsequent relationship of convenience with a charming Anglo-Irishman who secretly kept a mistress on the side. No wonder that she is so preternaturally alive to the unreliable streak in the plausible Karl; or that she, a childless woman in later middle age, should be besotted by the supposed innocence of Meg and unreasonably concerned to protect her from the scheming clutches of men. All the stolid caution and resigned stoicism of his hill-farming ancestors are manifest anew in the Rector's actions. Colonel Bacon over-compensates with pseudo-military bluster and comically inflated self-importance for his pre-war civvy-street work as 'manager of a small town branch of the Halifax Building Society'. (*US*, 20)

Then there are the sexual elements in the mix. There is more than a hint of repressed lesbian desire in the Countess's exceptionally intense fascination with Meg's young beauty and her 'strange desire to see her small again, so that I could spend my day fondling and stroking her'. (*US*, 89) Olwen takes her husband aback by frankly discussing the difference between male and female sexuality, in the process pointedly admitting that even the most staid and respectable of married women cannot be denied their transgressive sexual fantasies. The impressionable and highly suggestible young Meg is easily seduced sexually by Klaus, and this instantly alters her social and political outlook. As, therefore, is the case in so many of Humphreys's novels, sexuality is here a far more insidiously powerful and comprehensive driver of the action than the narrative chooses openly to acknowledge.

Biting satiric comedy is also very much part of the mix in *Unconditional Surrender*, and it is distributed liberally and evenhandedly. The Gethin-Wynnes are types instantly recognisable to the Countess, whose beady eyes immediately see that 'in spite of their names and their ancestry [theirs] was a class of Sudeuten English marooned on their properties, fortified with nick-names and illustrated magazines'. (*US*, 69) Hosting a polite *soirée*, 'Garnett Gethin-Wynne was helpful and charming . . . His pink bow tie and his ivory cigarette-holder signalled his devotion to culture.' (*US*, 70) The local Plaid Cymru candidate, a gangling scholar eagerly supported by Meg, is summarily dismissed by the Rector (who is anxious to avoid commitment by discrediting him) as 'a tall, thin restless fellow who needed a lot of elbow room. He had this torrential no-time-to-waste South Wales way of talking that would be more of a hindrance than a help in this constituency.' (*US*, 57) Likewise, the Rector acidly remarks on how '[we knew] all about Griff's conscience. We all did. At this very moment it was being inflated like an air balloon in the centre of our kitchen.' (*US*, 32) As for the Colonel, even though his war service has been exclusively confined to managing transport arrangements he is given to 'affecting an even more nasal twang to lend additional *sang froid* to his anecdote[s]'. (*US*, 71)

The series of farcical actions that accumulate as the novel draws to its conclusion hover between pathos and tragedy. Roused by the treachery of his 'friend' Klaus in making Meg pregnant, Griff hurls a pitchfork but succeeds only in wounding him in the shoulder. Determined at least to revenge herself on Colonel Bacon, who is engineering her transportation back to Germany, the Countess sets out to kill him with a bullet from a shotgun, but manages only to wound herself instead. The Rector believes he can shock his wife Olwen into her 'senses' by revealing Meg's pregnancy only to discover she is already aware and calmly unperturbed. As to his idyllic illusion that he can at least find relief and consolation from the appalling revelations about the Concentration Camps by returning to work on his family farm, that is shattered when Griff's violent attack on Klaus in a barn underlines the fact that rural life has ever been full of a ruthless bloody struggle for survival. And all these desperate and futile actions seem to be very much in keeping with the results of the recent 1945 General Election that have returned Labour to power and confirmed that the nationalist movement has completely failed to rouse the Welsh people out of their torpor and inertia. The whole world may be changing, but here in Wales everything can be safely relied upon to remain exactly the same as ever.

As for Meg, it is because of her feelings of hopeless disgust at such a prospect that – and here the tone of the novel turns bitterly ironic – she actually believes a better future must await her with the plausible, unreliable Klaus in a defeated and totally ruined Germany where, as the Rector bleakly realises as he looks at the pictures:

> Bremen is a waste land licked by a black river. The ruins of Nürnberg stretch over two pages like a bloated corpse being eaten by blind worms. There is no noise of explosion, but the centre of Cologne has become a black and white catastrophe. Broken bridges sag and sink into water that has lost the ability to flow. Railway tracks bend and buckle into the ground like a shower of arrows aimed at the devils in hell. (*US*, 93)

As if to make absolutely sure that the Rector's miseries are complete, his wife Olwen heads off for a taste of the 'wicked world' in the company of Colonel Bacon, confident that, like her daughter

Meg, she has the makings of a 'survivor.' Finally comes the news about a 'single bomb that has vaporised an entire city in Japan'. (*US*, 153)

But then, ambivalent as ever, the novel ends by noting that the Rector's son Eryl has been commended and promoted in North Africa, and that his wife and daughter are busy working as volunteer workers in a training centre for refugee work. And having found refuge anew in the largely vacant Rectory, the Countess determines to help the Rector complete his history of the parish. Although sympathetically treated, the choice made by Olwen and Meg are the diametric opposite of the one made by Humphreys himself at the very same point in history. It is therefore as if, at the age of seventy seven, he has chosen to look way back over the five intervening decades to assess an option that had been available to him at that time but had not been accepted. This makes *Unconditional Surrender* a valedictory *apologia pro vita sua* that is rather moving.

* * *

Unconditional Surrender is quite a short novel, its themes as intricately worked and interwoven as in a fugue. As such, it has much in common with the novella and three collections of short stories Humphreys fashioned as he advanced deeper into old age. But his very next work was a full-scale novel in which themes are again interlaced bewilderingly, with all the tightness and elaborateness of a Celtic knot. The two main protagonists of *The Gift of a Daughter* are Dr Aled Morgan, a middle-aged Classicist turned Archaeologist, through whose eyes everything and everybody in the novel are viewed, and his wife Marian. Both were language activists in their ardent youth, but now, in the opinion of their beloved late teenage daughter Rhiannon, a promising student at Cambridge, they have long become lamentably set in their ways. They are accordingly totally lacking in the adventure she herself craves and finds in the unsuitable company of a slightly ageing hippy, Buddy, an unsavoury character given to vague, New Age maunderings. Together they haunt megaliths, seeking from them some esoteric wisdom. Rhiannon's eventual lonely, bloody, death by miscarriage devastates her parents, who for the rest of the novel seek a variety of ways in which to deal with their agony of loss.

Rhiannon's lovingly exasperated rebellion against her parents' cautious conservatism mirrors, of course, not only Meg's reaction against her Rector father in *Unconditional Surrender*, but also similar child-parent conflicts in several of Humphreys's other novels. And her mother Marion's gradual, growing empathy with her daughter's viewpoint to the confusion of Aled is not dissimilar to the empathic bond between Olwen and Meg from which the Rector increasingly discovers himself to have been excluded. Here, then, are two of the main themes that recur in Humphreys's fiction: that of intergenerational conflict and of deep, instinctive female solidarities. Linked to the latter is Humphreys's respect for the core toughness of women – so many of his female characters are paired with, if not indeed yoked to, males incapable of matching them in spirit and potency, as is the case in the increasing tense marriage of Marian and Aled. Also extensively and variously explored in *The Gift of a Daughter* are the respective claims of past and present on the lives of individuals and societies alike. The past that threatens to dominate and overpower the Morgans's present is not only their unforgettable past with Rhiannon but also, in the case of Aled the academic, the past of the Italy of both Etruscan and Classical times, in both of which he supposes he detects useful parallels to his own present situation.

The Gift of a Daughter is undoubtedly the most intensely European of all of Humphreys's novels, not least because around half of the action is located on the Continent. Italy is the refuge to which Aled and Marian repair in the aftermath of their unbearable loss, drawn by the imposing figure of Aled's old friend, Muzio. He is a decayed aristocrat of impeccable manners, considerable learning, and wealth of weary and wary worldly experience such as only life in a country as ancient and as chronically and cynically steeped in intrigue as Italy would, it is implied, be capable of producing. One of Muzio's interests is Etruscan remains, a subject that had come to fascinate

Humphreys in his later years because Basil MacTaggart, his oldest and closest friend since their days together running the Displaced Persons Camp, had become an amateur expert on Etruscan civilisation, having settled permanently in Italy after the war.

Another theme examined in *The Gift of a Daughter*, as in several of Humphreys's other works – most notably *The Anchor Tree* – is the magnetic attraction of beautiful young women for men in their middle years. That attraction is a complex compound of sexual desire for young flesh and a nostalgia for innocent youthful idealism – although in every fictional treatment of the case by Humphreys the young female subject of middle-aged adoration turns out to be far more experienced and canny than her gullible admirer supposes. The young girl in question in Aled's case is Grazia, from Muzio's district, whom the Welshman soon comes to conflate with Rhiannon. Marion, too, becomes enchanted with her, and equally inclined to project on to her the supposed qualities not only of her late lamented daughter but also of her own youthful self.

Both husband and wife are led to construct a heroic narrative that involves plucking Grazia from the clutches of her domineering father so as to provide her with the education that her intelligence deserves and that would grant her freedom to develop as she wishes. But the implementation of their somewhat histrionic plan – it involves subterfuge and disguise engineered by Prue, Muzio's no-nonsense English wife who is actually an opera singer – triggers another of the subjects that recur in Humphreys's fiction: the right to freedom of self-development that has become a cardinal principle of modern democratic Western society, versus the responsibility to respect and sustain your society and collective that is also an imperative if local cultures are to withstand the powerful forces of global homogenisation. A related theme is that of complete freedom of movement on the one hand and on the other the necessary defence of the boundaries without which distinctive societies and cultures cannot continue to exist. Grazia's story, as it unfolds, allows Humphreys to investigate such matters very subtly. There is a hint, though, of the crafty Machiavellian Italy of some of Henry James's great fictions in this treatment by Humphreys of Italian culture.

As for the bearing the history of ancient Rome has on these contemporary proceedings, that emerges from Aled's growing interest in that period in the sixth century when the Byzantine Emperor Justinian and his controversial Empress Theodora, who had originally been a courtesan of low birth, were seeking to reclaim control of Rome from Theodosia, daughter of Theodoric, a Goth-turned-Roman. Aled sees a parallel in this situation to the way he thinks the USA is seeking to impose its power on the Old Countries of Europe. But he also slowly begins to identify himself after a fashion with Procopius. Sometime obedient scribe to Justinian, the official had turned against his master in his later years and written a bilious and notorious *Secret History* of his time, full of lubricious details about the scandalous antics of both Justinian and the libidinous Theodosia. Procopius is thus presented by Humphreys as a rogue variant on the Dissident figure he has always so admired.

For a period, Aled fancies himself to be, like Procopius, an undercover agent secretly working to undermine and expose the moral corruption he slowly detects in Italy. This decadence is apparent in the torrid affair that Prue, Muzio's wife, is openly conducting with the priapic Luzio, who is Muzio's secret half-brother and irresistibly macho estate manager. And it is differently evident in the violence Grazia's father is willing to exert to maintain his domination over his cowed family and clan. Even Muzio himself is gradually realised by Aled to be sexually impotent and accordingly complaisant in his wife's affair. As for Muzio's mother, an ancient, heavily bejewelled Marchese, the viciously scheming old crone is a survivor from the Mussolini era and therefore as well used to being socially and politically complaisant as her son is to being sexually obliging.

But by the end of the novel it has become evident that Aled is not remotely up to remedying weaknesses that are not peculiar to Italy but in many respects inherent in the human condition. As his wife – who has turned out to be considerably more pragmatically resourceful and effective than he in handling the situation – remarks to him with a mixture of sympathy and condescension, he is much too gentle a soul to survive even in the world of intricately devious family politics in which he has become entangled in Italy. Following her advice, Aled therefore returns to Wales and to his first love, *De Consolatione Philosophiae* ('*The Consolation of Philosophy*'), written in prison in the early sixth century by the politician-turned-philosopher Boethius, after he had been sentenced to death by the Emperor he had once loyally and obsequiously served.

* * *

Although there is a gap of seven years between the publication of *The Gift of a Daughter* and that of Humphreys's latest novel to date, *The Shop*, the latter shares some settings and preoccupations with the former. For instance, just as a substantial part of *The Gift of a Daughter* relates to Italy, so in *The Shop* an early part of the action occurs in the Alentejo region of Portugal, and includes a visit to the cromlechs at Almendres (not Almendras, as the novel has it). And just as Humphreys had been introduced to Etruscan culture by his friend Basil MacTaggart, long resident in Italy, so had he been introduced to Portugal by his brother, who had spent his later years as chaplain to the Anglican community there.

The Shop also features a first-person narrative and its main pro-tagonist, too, is a young academic. Eddie (full name Edward Lloyd) is son of a Swiss mother and a Welsh father – Orlando Lloyd (full name Hubert Cynddylan Vaughan-Lloyd), sometime matinee idol, grand Shakespearean actor of the old school of rhodomontade, and blithe, aged philanderer. He is of course, a late addition to Humphreys's acid portrayals of louche theatrical and media types, just as Eddie Lloyd is another of his examples of rather ineffectual young Welsh males liable to be dominated by strong females. The resentful son, a 'burgeoning international bureaucrat', (*S*, 50) camps in a gloomy flat in Rome while his ineffably self-regarding and condescending father, although reliant on his son's financial sup-port, is comfortably holed up in a luxurious apartment in fashion-able Juan-les-Pins, coastal resort and spa in Antibes.

There are also interesting instances of reversal of theme between the two works. Both, for example, feature young women anxious to escape their stifling home environments, but whereas that environment is traditional Italian culture in *The Gift of a Daughter* it is that of a Welsh-language home and Welsh-language schooling in *The Shop*. Both are shown to be equally capable of quelling independence of mind and spirit. And Bethan Mair Nichols, a stills photographer working with documentary film units and the young woman in question in the latter novel, is, like Grazia, one of the last in a long line stretching back at least as far as Lydia, the frustrated wife of J.T. in *Outside the House of Baal* and the Amy Parry of the *Land of the Living* sequence. All of these were ambivalent studies by Humphreys of the descendants of the liberated New Woman of the 1920s.

As the story unfolds, the novel homes in on one of his most urgently recurring themes, already encountered in *The Gift of a Daughter*: the ambivalent relationship of the young – particularly in Wales – to ancestral home, family and culture, balanced against their generation's fiercely asserted right to unfettered freedom of personal development wherever that might lead. In the case of the increasingly rootless Eddie, who has never visited Wales, this takes the form of initially cautious exploration of reputedly grand family ties with the Welsh Marcher Lords. The most ruthlessly opportunistic and astute of these had become gratefully assimilated into the English aristocracy, while the rest had sunk down into membership of the mediocre middle class. Eddie is enticed into these explorations by his lover, Bethan Mair, a *soi-disant* liberated young woman who initially proposes to adopt a cool, professional, and slightly cynical attitude towards the exploration of her own Welsh family background, only to become absorbed with increasingly dangerous intensity in the whole enterprise.

Bethan Mair is jadedly familiar with the threat of global culture to distinctive local communities worldwide. Humphreys thus preempts criticism that he is unwittingly dealing in stale materials; and indeed by means such as these he even brings an ironic touch of knowingness to bear on his narrative, although not to the usual postmodern effect of relativising and thus effectively invalidating any set convictions but rather to imply defiantly that it is not through a lack of self-awareness that he continues to cherish the values to the service of which he has devoted his whole long life and career. Thus, for instance, one of the characters refers passingly to 'the Welsh condition', implying that Bethan Mair may end up enthralled by it. By that time, her resolution not to be affected by her family's claustrophobic concern with the future of the Welsh language and the communities it has traditionally sustained has begun to falter. This is the outcome of what had been intended to be no more than a professional 'reccy' to visit with Eddie a property inherited through her maternal aunt.

Once the thriving traditional centre of what is now a decaying Welsh rural village near the English border, the ramblingly spacious Pentregwyn General Stores is as good as derelict, its only inhabitant a kind of amiable squatter, Curig Huws, who is a lost soul, sensitive and gentle. It is, though, only after reading a letter left for her by a deceased great-aunt, the store's last owner, that Bethan Mair begins to be hypnotised by the place and what it represents both to her family and for Welsh-language culture. This letter is lengthy and interesting, though it does rather obtrude as an obvious, awkward narrative device and its effect on Bethan Mair is transformative, throwing her clean 'off her rational keel', as Eddie exasperatedly opines. (S, 102)

The acidity level of Eddie's narrative increases dramatically from this point on, as he senses his lover drifting away into the company both of ghosts and of 'mystic Curig' (S, 113), whom he christens a kitchen anchorite. But that acidity spills over to powerful effect onto the other significant characters in his life, most notably his outrageously theatrical father, long given to adopting an 'Old Boy' personality, mixing acquired public-school slang with that of his fellow-luvvies of the theatrical profession, and enthusiastically playing the part of a robust English jingoist, bullish Eurosceptic and royal-worshipper. This late novel includes extensive social comedy as cuttingly satiric any in Humphreys's previous fiction.

Another of Eddie's acquaintances who represents the new, cynical pan-European élite of international civil servants and media hustlers, as much at their ease in Denmark as in Rome, in France as in Spain, is his line manager Freddy Helmut, originally from Germany. At one juncture Eddie perceptively styles him a modern Lord of Misrule, and contrasts him with the man he most admires, Father Afonso. He is a gently self-effacing Franciscan monk and therefore also a world-traveller, but one devotedly serving as 'the apostle of a higher form of law and order'. (S, 158)

The intermingled worlds of theatre and media production, of both of which Humphreys has had extensive personal experience, are subjected to sustained examination in this novel, much of it brilliantly hostile. Bethan resumes contact with those worlds when she flirts with the idea sold to her by Jens, a pretentious Danish director. He proposes to make a documentary about the interesting life of her aunt Sulwen, who had had a secret lover. But balancing this caustic portrayal of media types is the personality of Daisy. Seeming at first to be no more than a faded stage actress still theatrically clinging to the vestiges of youth and beauty, she turns out to be thoroughly decent, and proves to be a selfless carer for her new husband Orlando Lloyd when the roguish Old Fruit is finally felled by a stroke.

Melodrama conveniently intervenes – not for the first time, as we have seen, in Humphreys's fiction. Bethan Mair is badly injured when a criminal gang raid the property, their interest having been aroused by Jens's tall tales about Hollywood money being invested in Pentregwyn Stores. In attempting to protect her, Curig Huws is left in an even worse condition. The time he spends in intensive care seals Bethan Mair's conviction that the rehabilitation of the General Stores is inseparable from the rehabilitation of Curig. And so, once she has recovered, she resumes – this time with the guarded, sceptical support of Eddie, who has been summarily recalled to her side – her mission to convert the old shop for modern use and make it the vibrant regenerative centre of what remains of the local community. Part of her grand design involves marriage to Eddie.

This late novel, however, turns out to be one of Humphreys's most unexpectedly searching and sceptical investigations of the possibility of implementing the kind of adaptive initiatives he continues to believe are necessary if a Welsh culture is to survive. *The Shop* therefore ends not with the expected success of Bethan Mair's enterprise, but with her sudden departure to take advantage of a wonderful commission to help make 'a series of documentary films on the present state of racial and class relations in seven major English cities'. (*S*, 223) So who is left to mind the shop? Who but Eddie, whom she has recently married. Equally recent is his reluctant recruitment as supporter of her ambitious scheme for the Stores. So what, given Bethan Mair's abrupt departure, are the chances of the long-term survival of either the marriage or the scheme itself?

The implications of such an unexpected ending are intriguingly complex. It is as if, having crossed the threshold of eighty, Humphreys has developed a disillusioned Euroscepticism of his own distinctive kind. Because what has emerged is not the Europe of rich cultural diversity he had imagined, but a Europe that is becoming one vast playground for the pampered and privileged élite of mobile 'internationalists', disseminators of the powerful new monoculture of global technology. By the same token, Bethan Mair is sadly revealed to have been at bottom nothing but the Amy Parry of a new age. The high road away from Wales to London and English assimilation had been for Amy, as for all the many generations before her since Tudor times, the high road to wealth, power, and social recognition. So, too, for Bethan Mair, except that for her modern generation the future lies beyond not only Wales but also England, in the direction of whatever green pastures media cameras can discover in the culturally undifferentiated landscape of Europe. And despite her loudly-voiced misgivings about the theatrical falsifications of the media industry, Bethan Mair has, it seems, been re-producing all along in her imagination nothing but a stagey, folksy version of traditional Welsh village life.

And there is one final important aspect of *The Shop* that links it firmly to Humphreys's previous fiction. In this novel, once more, references to old Welsh legend and literature are used, almost imperceptibly, to calibrate the actions and experiences of the present. There are three examples to note. First, the epigraph, from the

Mabinogion tale of 'Pwyll Pendefig Dyfed': 'Ac fe debygai ef y'i goddiweddai ar yr ail naid neu ar y drydedd. Er hynny nid oedd yn nes ati na chynt.' 'He assumed that at the second bound or at the third he would overtake her. Yet he drew no closer to her than before.' Having glimpsed sight of the beautiful Rhiannon a short distance ahead, Pwyll, Prince of Dyfed, supposes he can easily draw abreast of her, only to discover that however quickly he moves the distance between them never lessens, although the lady herself never quickens her pace. Obviously an allusion to Eddie's pursuit of the endlessly elusive Bethan Mair, it also suggestively applies to Emyr Humphreys's lifelong attempt, in his novels, to get the measure of the many intriguing female characters he has himself created.

Another significant allusion relates to the name 'Cynddylan', bequeathed to Eddie by his father. Its implications are made explicit when Bethan Mair quotes the famous lines from a great tenth-century poem: 'Ystafell Cynddylan ys tywyll heno' ('Cynddylan's hall is dark tonight'.) The lines describe the great hall of a powerful Welsh chieftain of the March, that has been laid waste by powerful forces from what would become the English side of Offa's Dyke. Their relevance to the state of Pentregwyn Stores and of the community it used to serve is therefore evident.

Less obvious, but if anything even more hauntingly effective, are the resonances of lines that briefly occur to Eddie, who has been introduced to them by Bethan Mair: 'shame on my beard if I don't open this door to see if what they said about it is true'. (*S*, 60) They are spoken by Heilyn mab Gwyn in a *Mabinogion* tale. Retreating from Ireland with the head of the mighty Bran, seven Welsh warriors find refuge on the island of Gwales (the modern Grassholm, off the Pembrokeshire coast). There they are assured of magical protection from all manner of woes and sorrows, but only for as long as they refrain from opening one fateful door that faces towards Cornwall. Of course, as these lines indicate, Heilyn mab Gwyn just cannot resist defying such a prohibition, with the result that he opens the door and lets in a whole world of devastation. It is a story that ominously foretells the fate that is to befall poor Eddie himself, once he has allowed Bethan Mair to open the door of Pentregwyn Stores that gives on to all the over-whelming and seemingly insoluble problems that sadly beset contemporary Wales. But it also clearly applies to Emyr Humphreys himself, who in opening the door facing on to the Welsh scene by writing *The Shop* has found himself faced with a deeply disturbing prospect for the future.

* * *

Since entering his eighties in 1999, Emyr Humphreys has published three substantial collections of stories: *Ghosts and Strangers* (2001), *Old People are a Problem* (2003) and *The Woman at the Window* (2009), which was published when Humphreys had reached his ninetieth year. Some of these stories are long and complex and might therefore be alternatively classified as novellas. Humphreys has interesting views on both the short story and novella forms. In his view, his repeated use of episodic structure in his novels has meant that his imaginative resources for the short story form – the 'flash of revelation of . . . [a] small moment' (*CR*, 180) – have become 'exhausted'. Hence his preference for the novella, a form practised with distinction not only by Kate Roberts in some of her stories, but also by renowned Continental authors such as Flaubert in his *Trois Contes* and Chekhov in his longer short stories. (*CR*, 183)

As for the contemporary Wales depicted in the novellas in *Ghosts and Strangers*, it is a world away from that known to little Amy Parry, growing up in the desperately poor hillside cottage of Swyn-y-Mynydd after the First World War; or to Albie, Michael and Iorwerth as they struggled to survive a provincial upbringing under the shadow of the next, impending, war; or to Pen Lewis, Communist organiser in the Rhondda during the depression 1930s, who died young, victim both of his war-torn age and of its violently conflicting ideologies; or to the minister J.T. who lived on into old age in the early 1960s only to become agonisingly aware of the wreckage all around him of his Nonconformist values and beliefs. Humphreys, a veteran of all these preceding decades, has remained sufficiently alert and intellectually flexible in his old age to realise that for him the present is now a foreign country: they do things differently here. And he has also remained imaginatively resourceful enough to be able to devise convincing fictional means of mapping this strange contemporary territory.

That he has been able to do so is, perhaps, due in no small part to two considerations. First, for all its undoubted strangeness to Humphreys's ageing eyes, an erstwhile proletarian Wales has become, in its post-industrial form, primarily home to a middle class the development of which by stages throughout the twentieth century has long been his main subject. It is a middle class that enjoys a comfortable standard of living and ease of international travel and this has enabled it to treat the whole of Europe as its own backyard and leisure playground. Needless to say, this is nothing like the Europe of rich regional diversity and 'local' cultural sophistication that has long been dreamt of by Humphreys the lifelong Europhile: he has, after all, always taken his cue from the Saunders Lewis who had been devoted to a vision of a robustly bicultural Wales reclaiming its rightful place, as the last surviving heir of the Roman Empire, in the great sophisticated civilisation of continental Europe. Much of Humphreys's later fiction explores the gap between his high aspirations and this dispiriting reality.

The second fundamental feature of Humphreys's outlook that has enabled him to retain his imaginative grip on Welsh experience throughout the changeful decades is that definitively outlined in *The Taliesin Tradition*. He has remained convinced that there are deep aspects of the Welsh psyche that, for better and for worse, continue, Taliesin-like, to survive even the most radical of changes in superficial Welsh circumstances. And it is these abiding aspects that he has chosen to address in his three late collections of short stories.

One of the most prominent, and perhaps chronic, characteristics of the settled Welsh mentality is an anxiety to please; an endless obligingness. Seemingly ingrained in the psyche, it is seen by Humphreys as the inevitable consequence of initial conclusive defeat followed by centuries of colonial subordination. And, as many cultural commentators have pointed out, it is a condition that has been repeatedly reinforced by such notoriously demeaning episodes in Welsh history as the 1847 Government Report into the state of education in Wales. Infamously labelled the 'Treachery of the Blue Books', it branded the Welsh people almost universally immoral, and treated 'ignorance' and 'ignorance of the English language' as if they were synonymous. For a half century and more thereafter the Welsh tried desperately to prove to their English neighbours that theirs was a code of conduct every bit as lofty as that of Victorian England, and cultivated a reputation for musical talent to demonstrate how highly civilised their nation was.

In 'Ghosts and Strangers', the lead character, Gwion Lloyd Roberts, is a striking study in Welsh deferentiality. A naturally stolid character, he has contentedly spent most of his life working as a gardener on the landed estate of Lord Pascant. But then in middle age he unexpectedly and disconcertingly finds himself owner of the entire property, following the death of his wife Rowena, who had previously been the Lord's widow. But while he is thus set free by her largesse to wander the Continent and visit some of its great historic gardens, he remains psychologically unchanged, still helplessly anxious as only a born servant could be to please whatever chance stranger happens to appeal to his good nature. Exploited first by Simon Huff, a blusteringly blunt teacher from Yorkshire and a self-styled poet who refers to Gwion contemptuously as 'Welshy', and then by the ersatz poet's self-dramatising lover, he ends up pathetically offering to support the young family Huff has cavalierly abandoned, only to be angrily rebuffed by the Yorkshireman's firmly self-sufficient wife. To the end, he has proved every bit as 'pliable', 'ingratiating', and 'eager to please' as the hard-nosed Sol shrewdly judges the Welsh to be in 'Glasshouses', a story from *Old People Are A Problem*. (*OPP*, 223)

One concern that has spanned Humphreys's entire lifetime as a writer has been the ambivalent consequences for modern Wales of the claims the country's long past continue to make on its present. In 'Ghosts and Strangers' the negative effects of this spectral past are evident in Gwion's actions, inhibited as he is at every turn by awed recollections of his late wife's forceful advice. She had been much the stronger partner in their relationship, thus in effect reducing her husband to that state of ineffectuality that has so often characterised Welsh men in Humphreys's fiction, suggesting that long suppression has made the country itself, like so many of its men-folk, incapable of acting decisively in its own interests. Even an apparently strong Welsh male such as the successful solicitor Arnot in 'Menna' turns out to live a life not only haunted by the death of his twin in early childhood but also effectively governed by the neurotic demands of his artist-wife, Lisa. Moreover, the alliance she slowly and almost imperceptibly forms with Arnot's mother, Menna, is a late example of another recurrent feature of Humphreys's fiction: intimate friendships between women to the virtual exclusion of the men in their lives. Very rarely are his male characters able to match the strength of character, determination of will, or sheer resilience of his female characters.

So powerful, indeed, are some of the women in his fiction that they can seem more sinister than impressive. Particularly when their power is exerted during the course of one of those tense struggles between the sexes that abound in his novels, where the women usually turn out to be much more ruthlessly clear-sighted than the men. Even Llinos, outwardly ever the self-disciplined, morally upright character suggested by her nickname of 'Lady Ramrod' (in the story of that name), discovers under provocation an unexpected atavistic violence within her equal to that of her physically violent husband.

But much more disturbing is the case of the sardonically sadistic Malan, in 'Penrhyn Hen', renowned locally as the soul of respect-ability and for her devotion to 'cleanliness and service'. (GS, 153) Having lured her younger sister, Sioned, home on a mercy visit, she then traps her into permanent care for Malan's husband, Ritchie, who has been comprehensively disabled by a serious fall precip-itated by his vengeful wife. In Malan's bitter, perverted mind, Ritchie's fate and Sioned's plight are their appropriately doomed joint 'inheritance'; just biblical retribution for the affair they had briefly enjoyed many years before. Moreover, Malan's consequently dark obsession with sin is the reverse of that naively innocent belief in human goodness that had characterised her in her youth, when hers had been that wilfully gullible outlook on life now cultivated by Sioned's lover, Bryn, who ends up because of it victimised and shockingly disabused. Both Bryn and Malan in her youthful form are thus late additions to the long gallery of innocents in Humphreys's fiction. All of these represent in part those escapist, self-emasculating aspects of the Welsh psyche that are the product of the final phase of Welsh Nonconformity; a post-Calvinist phase that saw it become so soggy with sentimentality that it was no longer capable of fully facing up to the real challenges of human life.

Malan's actions are also an attempt to lock Sioned in with her past; to make her permanently answerable to nothing but her personal and family history; to underline the fact that she can have no future separate from it – any more than could the baby, born of her unwilling union with Ritchie, whom Sioned had chosen to abort, thus denying her sister that future she believed she could have enjoyed by raising it. And at the story's end, Sioned un-expectedly embraces the vision so ominously if stylishly mapped out for her in her late sister's compelling diaries. Whether Sioned's actions are as wholly volitional and fulfillingly liberating as to her they seem is left deliberately open at the end.

The drag of the past on the present – a drag inhibiting in its effects and yet not entirely without its disturbing overtones of righteous rebuke – is powerfully examined in 'Old People are a Problem', in which a crabby old spinster, Keturah Parry, enrages her exasperated family by setting up camp in Soar, a chapel that has become distinctly surplus to local needs. Keturah – who, at ninety three, is only some five years older than Humphreys was when he wrote this story – has lived tetchily on to see her grand-daughter gallivanting off to places like Genoa on protest demon-strations and bringing home for refuge an Italian girl and her child born out of rape. She has also survived to see her nephew marry into the family of a 'turncoat' who had prospered financially and socially decades earlier by turning Anglican and exploiting the local workforce. It is through the complex interaction between the members of this single extended family who represent very different eras, backgrounds, experiences and values that Humphreys works out his ambivalent attitude towards the gains and losses of Welsh modernity's blithe indifference to its past.

Slyly puncturing old Keturah's determinedly rosy view of the chapel past is the sliver of information unearthed by Twm Moi, a colourfully rebellious young man, who discovers that in the distant past a heretically-inclined young minister had been forced to flee the locality after making the chapel organist pregnant. A similarly unvarnished community history is recorded in 'Before the War' by the engaging Elsie Probert, a spinster resident in Sheltered Accommodation. Whereas her young great-niece, Non, had expected to capture idyllic recollections on tape, Elsie finds herself instead thankfully shedding her inhibitions by frankly, if rather ruefully, recalling all the family tensions and local indiscretions that have lain safely concealed in her memory well into her eighties. Far therefore from being confirmed as the liberated and enlightened representative of the present, the well-travelled young Non comes to realise that her great-aunt, a stick-in-the mud whose travels have never extended further afield than Liverpool, has amassed a very much greater store of worldly wisdom than herself. As is always the case in Humphreys's fiction, the pendulum of judgement keeps swinging ceaselessly between fidelity to the past and complete participation in the present, never conclusively settling in favour of either.

Humphreys never simplifies or sentimentalises when dealing with the issue of the past, partly perhaps because of his experience of the traumatic state of post-war Europe with its vast armies of displaced persons. That experience left him with understanding of the urgent need felt by so many at that grim time to escape the past by forgetting it so as to start over anew. Such memories operate within Humphreys to counterbalance and qualify his understanding of the totally different situation in Wales, where a decisive break with the past could well signal the end of any distinctive cultural identity, even while an obsession with it could disable the Welsh from meeting the challenge of present and future. It is the former state of willed amnesia, however, that receives his sympathetic attention in 'An Ethnic Tremor', a story in *Old People are a Problem* that features the journey reluctantly undertaken for the sake of her Welsh-American granddaughter, Megan, by Siri Lloyd to that northern region of Slovenia that had been occupied by German families such as her own before the war. There she comes painfully face to face with memories of her lover, a young Chetnik who was eventually caught and killed by Tito's forces.[1] It is an encounter the full force and import of which Megan, a typical young American whose interest in the past is purely academic rather than bred in the bone, naturally finds it impossible fully to comprehend. And Humphreys's sympathy for displaced persons, developed early, morphs easily into his late sympathy for refugees and asylum seekers like the Azerbaijani children whose company little Ruthie much prefers to that of her chillingly ambitious and indifferent parents in 'Looking after Ruthie', again from *Old People Are A Problem*.

Another prominent and ineradicable trait of the Welsh character clearly identified in *The Taliesin Tradition* is that provincial craving for the kind of social and financial success that has always been available only in London. A story repeated by every Welsh generation at least since Tudor times, it is played out in contemporary terms by Glyndwr Brace, who accordingly ends up as 'The Man in the Mist' in the story of that name from *Old People Are A Problem*. Affable and good-looking, Glyn has enjoyed a prominent television career in London until pressures both from within the changing world of broadcasting and from his ambitious pseudo-aristocratic wife and mother-in-law prompt him first to return to what initially promises to be a valued role in Welsh television and then, finally, on the collapse of his hopes, to a lone existence as shepherd in his original valley home in remote Welsh upland country.

It is a story Humphreys tells with a mixture of restrained pathos and acidic satire. Particularly biting are the sketches of the Central European mother-in-law, Lady Alma – 'Her black coiffure was in some disorder as she stood before me, her jewels flashing in the light of the chandeliers. For a moment her prominent teeth looked as aggressive as a crocodile's' (*OPP*, 86) – and of Kenneth Crosby-Jones, newly appointed Head of Programmes in Cardiff: 'He was a tall man with a roll in his gait that was sufficient to alert his staff that he had not taken on his new job in order to make their lives more comfortable.' (*OPP*, 94) The ever amiable Glyn, an incorrigible Welsh innocent at heart for all his acquired sophistication, stands very little chance of surviving the machinations of either.

* * *

'With Lord Parry of Penhesgyn there was no means of telling whether he was pleased to see you or pleased for you to see him.' This, the opening sentence of 'The Grudge', from Emyr Humphreys's last collection *The Woman at the Window* (2009), proves that at the age of ninety he had lost none of his edgy talent for the lapidary sentence or his appetite for acerbic insight into personality. In such viperish moments, he briefly allows himself to strike back at those many unattractive aspects of contemporary Welsh life he has, in real life, schooled himself to view with a necessary degree of equanimity.

Given indeed that Humphreys has somehow been able to maintain a remarkably cheerful composure in the face of changes that have virtually obliterated most of the features of the Welsh mental and social landscape he has himself most cherished, it is perhaps not surprising that his late stories contain many monitory examples of the contrary: of characters who grow old bitterly entrenched in a misplaced loyalty to what has gone beyond even the remotest possibility of return. Keturah Parry is one such character. But an even more unambiguous example is that of 'the crowned and chaired poet Gwilym Hesgyn' (*WW*, 19) in 'Grudge'. All the fury pent up in him over the years as everything he has achieved as an accomplished strict-metre poet becomes ever more casually devalued and ignored results only in a prostrating major stroke. By contrast, his hated cousin the ineffable Lord Parry of Penhesgyn, cruises effortlessly on, his sails serenely filled by the soft zephyrs of years of cumulative success in the English political system. And when his advances are rebuffed by his scornful cousin he retaliates in feline manner by insinuating to close confidantes that Gwilym has never forgiven him for once bailing him out of a rather embarrassing situation.

Humphreys chooses to bring this powerful late story to a bitterly and bitingly ambiguous conclusion. Having been felled by his stroke and rendered virtually mute, Gwilym Hesgyn is powerless to prevent the odious cousin he has so long kept at bay from visiting his bedside. Taking advantage of this opportunity for 'reconciliation', and presuming on the ties of their old, boyhood, friendship, Lord Parry duly turns up full of sympathy and bonhomie:

> [He] had been provided with a chair and sat holding the patient's emaciated hand in both his own. A rigid diagonal smile was fixed on Gwilym Hesgyn's face. They could see Lord Parry's eyes were watering.
> 'He recognised me', Lord Parry said. 'Straight away. No trouble at all.' (*WW*, 29–30)

For those familiar with the 'vocabulary of gesture' in Humphreys's fiction, it is a crucial scene redolent of so many others in his work likewise involving an equivocal clasping of hands, suggestive either of genuine conciliatory compromise with the powers that be, or a token, ironic submission to an inescapable reality that nevertheless remains totally unacceptable. It is a gesture that encapsulates Humphreys's long view of the chronic plight of Wales; the plight of a survival culture.

There is, therefore, a deep agony of apprehension at the very heart of all of Humphreys's writing that is all the more intense and poignant for his cool manner of dealing with it and for the confirmed determination of his publishers to avoid advertising it. Thus the blurb on the back cover of *The Woman at the Window* carefully desanitises the text by depoliticising it and converting its 'message' into the most anodyne of universalist terms. Tastefully describing the stories as 'urbane' in character, it continues in like vein:

> His protagonists look back over the patterns of their lives and forward
> too, for the chance to untangle family relationships, rekindle lost loves,
> or find a home for themselves in familiar yet fresh surroundings, from
> Italy to Angelsey [*sic*].

As always, Humphreys is again in this collection fascinated with
the dilemma of how to position oneself in relation to what's gone.
It is a situation sharply etched with enigmatic precision in 'The
Woman at the Window', the woman being the relatively young
widow of a Welsh husband who had intrigued her partly because
of his penchant for what her unexpected visitor, Elwyn Anwyl, a
sometime associate of her late husband's, calls 'ancestor worship'.
Humphreys deploys what in English terms might be called the
comedy of manners to exquisite perfection in order to convey the
elaborate ritual of exchanges between the pair who are complete
strangers, totally indifferent to each other. The story concludes
with the coolly self-possessed widow effectively choosing to turn
away from the opportunities of the present and devoting herself,
for better or for worse, to excavation of whatever had mattered to
her husband. In other words, she opts to take her future orientation
from his past. Left standing at the window, in the very same stance
she had adopted when her unexpected visitor called, she is symbolically transfixed not by the 'prospect', but by what is already
beginning to command her inner eye. 'She looked as unperturbed
as the landscape she was staring at. He raised his hat and disappeared from view.' (*WW*, 45)

By contrast, and as if by way of therapeutic corrective, the very
next story, 'The Rendezvous', offers an almost cruelly unillusioned
view of the romantic folly of obsession with the past. In outline it
is a commonplace plot enough. An elderly Welsh headmaster, still
foolishly besotted with memories of the young girl he had adored
half a century earlier, arranges to meet her at an airport, only of
course to discover not only that she has become exceedingly wealthy
through a series of advantageous marriages and has aged – cheerfully yet shockingly – into an invalid, but also that his fantasy about
their furtively passionate past had in any case been based all along

on wilful misapprehension of what had actually happened. As so often in Humphreys's fiction it is the woman who emerges as much the stronger and more realistic character in this scenario, proving to be one of life's indefatigable survivors indulgently amused by the persisting sentimental naivety and ineffectuality of Welsh men of a certain background and era. It is a perspective underlined by the intrusion into the scene of plump, stout Mattie, another of his acquaintances of yore: 'She was dressed now in a flouncy black and yellow dress in anticipation of a summer that had not yet arrived and she settled in the seat opposite like a wasp on a choice piece of cake.' (WW, 55)

As happens elsewhere in Humphreys's fiction, the ineffectual Welsh male takes the form in another of these stories of a pretentious, effortlessly self-deluding artist. In 'The Comet', such is the sour, narcissistic Hefin, who is sustained in his seemingly idyllic Balearic retreat by the practical and resourceful Swiss Giselle and indulgently enabled to wage a permanent war against his successful father Bryn Tanat, an ageing, self-satisfied Welsh Labour MP. It is a story in which Humphreys distributes his satiric disdain fairly equally between the unattractive Welsh pair, in the process also bleakly mocking that concern for the welfare of the planet that he has himself always taken very seriously. The darker logic of the story is revealed in its ending, where Hefin, who has already contrived an 'accidental' blow to the head that conveniently rendered it impossible for him to collect his father from the airport, manages again to damage himself – this time possibly permanently – by falling, in a drunken stupor, over the edge of the parapet of the roof garden where he has just been reciting his bombastic 'poetic' elegy for all doomed planetary life. His, like that of Gwilym Hesgyn, is manifestly an impotently introjected rage of frustration; a self-destructive urge that implicitly leaves the story reflecting pessimistically on the Welsh condition.

The female survivor in 'Luigi', a sad, desolate sliver of a story, is Sylvana, a young Italian girl who quickly deploys her charms to seduce a British major in the dangerous aftermath of the final defeat of Mussolini and his grandiose legions. As for poor Luigi himself, something of an inoffensive local mammy's boy and Sylvana's would-be suitor, he is left the helpless, hapless victim of a Fascist 'cause' in which he never believed but which he had been forced to serve briefly and catastrophically because of family pressure. The story begins and ends with him seeking lonely shelter in a graveyard, a grim comment on the casual human debris of war. In his lonely, bewildered way, Luigi, the isolated fugitive, is a person as displaced as those Emyr Humphreys had looked after fifty years earlier in his Florentine camp.

And another story, 'Nomen', seems likewise to arise from Humphreys's revisiting of his experiences in shattered post-war Italy. In hovering between realism and fantasy, it is a work unlike any other published by Humphreys, and refrains even from locating its action in any precise time or occasion. It could, in a way, be as much about a post-nuclear situation as about post-war Italy, and its central character Nomen is, as his name suggests, a mysteriously nameless survivor who seems to have no other function save to act as the scapegoat who sacrifices his own life in the wan hope of keeping alive the possibility of goodness and selflessness in this cold, eerie, cruel world. It therefore reminds us of Humphreys's lifelong interest, as a writer, in the figure of the 'holy innocent', a central, recurrent figure in his treatment of the condition of Wales.

Just as Henry James developed a fruitful fascination with the fate of culpably innocent young Americans at large in a wily and cynical old Europe, so Humphreys has, in later life, developed an interest in the Welsh likewise newly let loose on the Continent. Many of them, too, travel dangerously encumbered by the remnants of a Puritan chapel culture that in its declining decades had cultivated its own innocent dreams and illusions about the duties and potentialities of human nature. They are accordingly ill prepared to encounter an Italy whose Catholicism is thin cover for an underlying pagan sensuousness and opportunism. Such is the basic scenario in 'Vennenberg's Ghost', a story featuring the mannered exchanges between Griffiths, a Welshman on the verge of retirement from the international civil service in Geneva, and his old friend, Marloff, a sophisticated White Russian well used to affectionately teasing him for his unreconstructed Puritan tendency to confuse morals with mores, and to rush to judgement where it would be wisest simply to maintain a knowingly objective protective distance. Together they contemplate the implications of a story Marloff relates concerning an attractive young rich German widow who ends up an alcoholic controlled by her priapic and amoral gardener, Mario, and his equally scheming wife, Giusi. By the end of the story, it is clear that in contemplating eventual retirement in their vicinity, Griffiths is in fact considering placing himself in an alien environment he as a Welshman would be ill-equipped to survive undamaged, for all his carefully acquired worldly sophistication.

Conscious of being similarly imperilled following the death of her masterful, effortlessly cosmopolitan husband, the elderly Dilys Myfanwy Macphail (née Roberts), another Welsh Nonconformist who has spent a married lifetime travelling the Continent in her husband's company, opts in 'Home' to retreat to the vicinity of her childhood idyll in pre-war rural Anglesey, her grandfather's old homestead Gelliwen. As her first-person narrative makes clear, Dilys is pliable and chattily loquacious. Quite comfortably set up, and safely embarked on an examination of her minister father's sermons and records of family traits, she develops a tentative interest in his insistence that the present needs to retain some trace of, and thus continuity with, the past to remain meaningful. She is both disconcerted and excited therefore to learn that her truculently rebellious young grandson, Gabriel, a total stranger to Wales as to family history, has suddenly announced his intention to visit in order to improve his acquaintance with both. However, having made such preparations as she can for his arrival, Dilys is disappointed to learn that he has headed off to India instead, having ventured only so far into Wales as Swansea, and become thoroughly disillusioned with its lack of significant singularity. '"Second-hand English," he said,' his mother reports over the phone: '"obsessed with rugby and being famous and getting their names in lights in the West End."' (*WW*, 161)

Affably optimistic and forgiving as always, Dilys tries to counter this discouraging revelation of the realities of contemporary Wales with her own conviction that she, at least, lives in a part of the country where it is possible to reconnect with the past, even if only in the form of her father's papers. But then young people close to her are savagely attacked on a Bangor street following a Welsh pop concert, and that illusion, too, is shattered beyond repair, leaving Dilys nevertheless still indefatigably intent on making her 'home' even in this unpromising contemporary environment. A typical Welshwoman, with a lifetime's experience behind her of making convenient accommodations to get by, she is undeterred by this latest crisis. As for Humphreys, this story again confirms that, even in extreme old age, he has lost none of the courage and honesty needed fully to confront the current, dispiriting situation of Wales.

As is patently evident in 'Home', most of the stories in *The Woman at the Window* deal with old age, treating its comic and ridiculous aspects every bit as unsparingly as they address its pathos and tragedy. In 'The Ring and the Book', for example, Humphreys reflects on such features of ageing as the telescoping of early and late life into a single curiously bifocal continuous present, the comi-tragedy of dementia, the surprisingly powerful return of youthful dreams and illusions (Thomas Hardy it was who noted with chagrin how unnervingly vulnerable even old age could be to experience 'the stirrings of noon tide'), and the compromises that can enable the flowering of unlikely final relationships. Then there are the performative aspects of old age to which Humphreys is also alive – Sir Robin Williams Price, the old gentleman in 'The Garden Cottage', is 'tall and very thin and showing off a little' (*WW*, 187) as he complacently flaunts his advanced years even as he shrewdly assesses the middle-aged pair standing before him, 'smiling at each other in a way that suggested they were still pleased in what they saw after twenty-five years of marriage'. (*WW*, 188) Sir Robin's own cruelly perceptive assessments of the pair – Idris, for example, has 'the protruding belly that went with good food and a sedentary occupation' (*WW*, 188) – are neatly balanced by theirs of him, as when he struggles to control his loose false teeth long enough to masticate his food. (*WW*, 190)

Of course, old age inevitably entails trafficking constantly – sometimes voluntarily, at other times involuntarily – with the past, always a hazardous enterprise, as we have repeatedly seen, in Humphreys's fiction. A recurrent feature of the collection is therefore a virtuosic set of late variations on this compelling theme, as retrospect rushes in to fill the vacuum left by the absence of meaningful prospect. 'There was always an unspecified goal', the eighty-year-old Tom Prichard mordantly notes in 'Three Old Men': 'it has turned out to be old age.' (*WW*, 203)

The view that Humphreys takes of the ageing process of individuals and a whole society alike in *The Woman at the Window* is at once disconcertingly unflinching and poignantly elegiac. And as can be the case with old age, many of the experiences recorded here are a curious mix of the rambling, the desultory, and the pointed – as when, in 'The Garden Cottage', the ritual of civil exchanges about life present and past between the elderly country gentleman Sir Robin and his two unexpected middle-aged visitors culminates in the quietly startling revelation that all the while the corpse of Sir Robin's wife has been lying in state in an adjoining room, awaiting the arrival of 'the ambulance and the police'. (*WW*, 198)Similarly, in 'Three Old Men', inconclusive ruminations about the end of life (in both senses of the phrase) are interrupted by their stumbling across an Irish prisoner on the run, whose unconvincing attempt to intimidate them leads to a brief excited flurry of concerted action that itself then peters out into peevish banalities.

Interested in the parallels and continuities that can constitute an individual life, these stories are also equally interested in the strange mismatches that can exist between people's past and their present, such that the former can seem puzzlingly unrelated to the latter. Humphreys's exposure to refugee experience in post-war Europe prompts him repeatedly to feature cases where individuals with quite an exotic Continental history fetch up sooner or later in life strangely marooned in Wales. So how, wonders a retired minister's adolescent grandson Ifan Roberts in 'A Little History', can an interest such as his in 'Cymric strict metres' possibly be reconciled with his girlfriend Zofia's family experience of life in Poland, Siberia, Palestine and London? The story tells the story of how that particular circle ended up satisfactorily squared – largely through a process of mutual adaptation powered by a belief that love alone is able to empower people to outface and survive the threats and absurdities of the modern nuclear world.

Such, then, is the powerful nexus of distinctive qualities that makes this final, mature collection of stories a quiet classic in a genre than can boast quite a distinguished place in the annals of modern Welsh literature.

7

CONCLUSION

A just evaluation of Humphreys's distinguished, multifaceted career is dauntingly difficult to achieve. There is after all in the whole of Welsh writing nothing remotely comparable to it in terms of longevity of output, historical reach, geographical breadth, thematic range or consistency of quality. His has undoubtedly been a unique achievement. As for characterising it, it is Humphreys himself who has usefully suggested it might all be considered, from one point of view, a species of border writing. Indeed, the documentaries he scripted for HTV during the 1970s included a series on such border writers as Geraint Goodwin (of the Newtown area in Montgomeryshire) and Arthur Machen (from Gwent). In placing himself in their company he has, however, in mind much more than his birth and upbringing in that liminal zone where Wales and England have traditionally met. He is thinking more particularly of his cultural positioning, as one for whom the survival of the Welsh language is a *sine qua non* of the persistence of a meaningful Welsh identity but who has spent a lifetime having to write about Wales in English. Such a deeply ambivalent positioning has had profound implications for his fiction. It has meant, for example, that he has had to develop means of communicating to monoglot English readers not just the surface realities of Welsh-language experience, but also its deep-structure of accumulated meanings and its elusive resonances of signification. In the process he has run the very real risk of alienating his Welsh-language and his English-language readers alike.

And then there are the cognate problems, confronting his conscience as much as his imagination, of writing about Welsh-language culture in the very tongue that has long been threatening to obliterate it. But then there are the benefits that are the obverse of these potential disadvantages. His deep misgivings about English can actually serve to heighten and sharpen his awareness of the power of that language, and thus help ensure that he deploy it with all the scrupulous care and sensitivity which a munitions expert exhibits when handling inherently 'unstable' explosive materials and devices. There is therefore always a palpable inner tension to his finely turned phrases and sentences that lends them a compellingly edgy energy.

Not that Emyr Humphreys himself would wish all his novels to be uncritically accepted as of equal quality. He has remarked on the relative 'immaturity' of much of his early fiction – however well it was received at the time of its publication – although he has added reasonably enough that 'there are qualities in them that are peculiar to the time when they were written. They have a validity and a kind of quality of permanence.' (*CR*, 52) He is thinking primarily of the set of novels he completed while living away from Wales, and unconcerned as yet to embrace Welsh experience in his writings. The watershed point of his career could, therefore, be said to have been reached when, on his return to Pwllheli, he produced *A Man's Estate*. Other early works such as *The Italian Wife* he tends now to criticise for 'having too much undigested material in it', and for relying 'too much on the attempt to follow the myth, the myth of Phaedra, and to drag it into the modern period'. (*CR*, 54) Similarly, he views *Hear and Forgive* as inadvertently clumsy in structure, rather like those early space-crafts that had ugly bits sticking out of them in numerous directions. Some of his later works might also be suspected of similar weaknesses – fascinating though *The Gift of a Daughter* may be, it does tend to multiply themes at the cost of overall coherence. There are also instances – particularly in the *Land of the Living Sequence* – when some characters (particularly south Walians, perhaps!) seem reduced to the restrictive dimensions of a stereotype. The depiction of even a major character like Pen Lewis flirts with such a weakness in places.

Many of the other weaknesses that occasionally mar his fiction seem to result from the ousting of the writer within him by the preacher. These two equally unyielding traits in his character have, after all, been locked in mortal conflict from the very beginning. He confesses to being a preacher manqué, and admits that his lovingly exasperated family have had to give up trying to school him out of the ingrained habit of seeking out opportunities for sermonising everywhere. There is the related impulse to didacticise. For all of Humphreys's great admiration of the Wittgensteinian admonition that less means more, he cannot always resist the impulse to spell things out. And despite his best intentions, some of the brief episodes that characterises his late narrative technique can, perhaps particularly in the *Land of the Living* sequence, perilously resemble simplistic moral allegories and improving emblems. But then it is the same inner preacher, often at his sternest, that has added substance, weight, and point throughout his career to his brilliantly epigrammatic encapsulations of characters and actions.

But as to the achievement of his fiction at its best, there can be no doubting its major status. He is, in essence, the great chronicler of that Welsh middle class that, having emerged from Nonconformity during the later decades of the nineteenth century, underwent a conversion to secular form in the early twentieth century that has allowed it to thrive, albeit in vulgarised form, even amidst the rubble of the chapels in a post-industrial Wales. It is a subject as deeply unfashionable as it seems hopelessly remote from current concerns, lacking as it does even the strange glamour that seems, for some, to attach to the decline of the erstwhile great coalfield society of the south Wales industrial valleys. And yet, as his work has convincingly demonstrated, it is a segment of recent Welsh social – and indeed political – experience that continues to have a bearing on our present, and to be rich in its implications for our understanding of the complex, compound nature of modern Welsh identity.

But his lifelong devotion to Wales should not be allowed to obscure his related commitment to a wider, European vision. He has consciously sought to develop into a European novelist in the distinguished tradition that contains major figures such as Thomas Mann, in the sense that he has generally been more interested in the social and existential life of ideas than in class manners and fine sensibilities. And while his writing could be loosely classified as 'realist' in character it is a description that requires immediate qualification. His is often, for instance, a 'mythic realism', as it is underpinned by a deep interest in the great archetypes differently embodied in myths, legends and major literary works. His ambition at the time was to use such materials as a means of calibrating the actions and occurrences of the present. In the earlier part of his career, it was to Greek and Roman exemplars and to the works of Shakespeare that he instinctively turned. But as his novels came increasingly to be preoccupied with what, in his striking and succinct study of Kate Roberts, he suggestively termed 'Welsh time', he began to draw on the rich store of indigenous Welsh mythic and literary materials, most particularly the remarkably fertile collection of tales that constitutes the legendary medieval corpus that has come to be known in English as *The Mabinogion*.

His realism could also be suggestively styled, as he has himself pointed out, a 'poetic realism' in that he has always attempted to engender 'an emotional charge which extracts some kind of poetry from the situation. The poetic element in the fiction is very important to me.' (*CR*, 55) He is on record as acknowledging a deep debt to Anton Chekhov for demonstrating so memorably in his writing that it is possible – and may often even be necessary – to achieve a 'realistic' (in the sense of convincingly mimetic) effect, by means of the high artifice of a cunningly mannered style of writing. Even when registering the movements of an individual mind, he chooses to do so in a manner closer to Shakespeare's soliloquies than to the stream of consciousness of a writer like James Joyce. His inner monologues are highly stylised distillations of the contents of consciousness. Equally notable a feature of his fiction is its sensuousness – a quality that has unfortunately received little attention in this short introductory study. This is a passage from his last work, *The Woman at the Window*:

It is half term. Cledwyn and Cyril have arrived to give Wil Hafan a hand in removing the overgrown pampas grass. There is a smell of autumn in the air and they are making a bit of a mess trampling the lawn in that corner of the garden. Wil has his little truck attached to the back of his car. He provides the boys with leather hedging gloves to transport those knifelike fronds and he wields a machete to excavate the roots of the massive clump. He will fill the gaping hole and leave a batch of raw soil where he intends to plant fuchsias. (*WW*, 157)

The suggestion made at the very beginning of this study – that the main subject of all Humphreys's best work is at bottom the condition of Wales -- should by now need no further confirmation. What may however need further emphasis is that he has always regarded the plight of Wales as offering a conveniently small and correspondingly manageable example of the great problem facing societies small and large the world over as they find themselves trapped in a powerful process inexorably intent on their gradual obliteration. It is an insight recently underlined in *The Fall of Language in the Age of English*, a study of the destructive global expansion of English by the Japanese novelist Minae Mizumura that has proved a sensational bestselling success right across the world. In it she shocked readers by arguing that the ancient and mighty culture and literature of Japan, no less, was now in danger of being gradually overwhelmed and choked by the continuing spread of the aggressively anglophone Americanised culture that was the dark twin of economic globalisation.

This is precisely what Emyr Humphreys has been arguing quietly and persistently through the medium of his fiction and through the example of Wales for the best part of the last seventy years. And indeed, in the latest of his recorded public interviews he has again emphasised that this process of vandalism is the cultural equivalent of that greedy process of despoliation of landscapes and natural resources that is also threatening to destroy mankind sooner or later. To realise this is, then, to realise that far from being no more than yesterday's author who has unfortunately lived on into sad irrelevance in today's world, Emyr Humphreys remains, even in his nineties, a novelist urgently relevant not only for our present time but for our sustainable future also. A concentration on Wales has for him always been in part a conscious means of addressing much wider issues: 'The long history of a small nation is a convenient receptacle for growing a culture that may enable us to diagnose with great accuracy notable ailments of the human condition.' (*CR*, 179)

As for the unique contribution he has made to Welsh culture, and his towering presence within it, that might be most appropriately summed up by remarks he has himself made about another author:

> Kate Roberts belongs to that select category of artists whose work emerges from a given landscape and society with the numinous power of a megalith or a stone circle. This is a status not easily achieved. It requires a combination of servitude and revolt which reflects the relationship between the artist and her society. In retrospect, it is the product of a lifelong struggle and a lifelong commitment: the unceasing urge to be both a free artist and a responsible member of a society under siege from hostile historical forces . . . Her achievement is the capacity to dominate the continuing consciousness of her tribe. (*CR*, 77)

While Humphreys would be the first to insist that his own relationship to Welsh life could never be as naturally 'embedded' as that of a Welsh-language writer of the past such as Kate Roberts, there is no doubt that it is a fidelity to his people very much akin to hers – a fidelity that has found expression in criticism and celebration alike – that has throughout his writing career been the bedrock on which his achievement (every bit as 'epic' in its way as that of Roberts herself) has rested so impressively, immovably and securely.

And while he has always emphasised that he is first and foremost a writer, his primary impulse being always to fashion language into story, he has also chosen, from the beginning to the end of his writing career, to dedicate his 'stories' to the maintenance of a nation that could be meaningfully identified as distinctively Welsh in character. 'In a time of trouble,' as he has himself written:

when the foundations are shaking, any literature calls out for a writer of genius. His pen must be the seismographic needle that will enable his people, both his own generation and their posterity, to increase their understanding and strengthen their capacity to endure the up-heavals with which their little world is afflicted. (*TT*, 52)

It is a very just and exact account of Emyr Humphreys's own accomplishment.

Notes

I

1. Saunders Lewis (1893–1985), poet, dramatist, literary and cultural critic, charismatic political leader, was the single most prominent and talented figure on both the cultural and the political scene in Wales in the twentieth century. Noted for being one of the founders, and long-term President, of Plaid Cymru (the national party of Wales), he cultivated controversy throughout his life, believing Wales needed to be galvanised into developing a backbone of independent thought and action. Such were his achievements as a revolutionary Welsh-language dramatist that, shortly before his death, he was nominated for the Nobel Prize in Literature.

2. Saunders Lewis, 'Welsh Literature and Nationalism', in Alun R. Jones and Gwyn Thomas (eds), *Presenting Saunders Lewis* (Cardiff: University of Wales Press, 1973), p. 142–144. It was first published in the *Western Mail*, 13 March, 1965.

3. 'Outline of a necessary figure', in M. Wynn Thomas (ed.), *Emyr Humphreys: Conversations and Reflections* (Cardiff: University of Wales Press, 2002), pp. 84–91.

4. Most of the biographical information in this section and throughout this study is drawn from two important sources: *Conversations and Reflections* and Arwel Jones, *Dal Pen Rheswm: Cyfweliadau gydag Emyr Humphreys*.

5. R. Tudur Jones (1922–1998). Among those of his works of particular relevance to Humphreys are *The Desire of Nations* (Llandybie: Christopher Davies, 1974); *Congregationalism in Wales* (Cardiff: University of Wales Press, 2004); and *Faith and the Crisis of a Nation: 1890–1914* (Cardiff: University of Wales Press, 2004).

6. See 'The Night of the Fire', *Conversations and Reflections*, pp. 92–122.

7. R. S. Thomas used exactly the same metaphor to describe his own situation in 'The Creative Writer's Suicide' (1978), in Sandra Anstey (ed.), *R. S. Thomas: Selected Prose* (Bridgend: Poetry Wales Press, 1983), pp. 61–66.

8   D. Myrddin Lloyd (1909–1981). During the course of his distinguished
     career, Lloyd published several books, including two volumes of essays
     by Emrys ap Iwan, a trenchant late-nineteenth-century 'postcolonial'
     thinker and precursor of Saunders Lewis: D. Myrddin Lloyd (gol.),
     Detholiad o Erthyglau a Llythyrau Emrys ap Iwan, 3 vols. (Aberystwyth:
     Y Clwb Llyfrau Cymreig, 1937–1940); *Emrys ap Iwan* (Cardiff: University
     of Wales Press, 1979).

9   Elio Vittorini (1908–66) was a leading Sicilian novelist and an outspoken
     anti-fascist: Leonardo Sciascia (1921–89) was a famous Sicilian novelist
     and another strong anti-fascist who also exposed the Mafia; Eugenio
     Montale (1896–1931), widely regarded as the greatest Italian poet since
     Giacomo Leopardi; Giuseppe Ungaretti (1888–1970), was an acclaimed
     Italian modernist poet; Luigi Pirandello (1867–1936), a Sicilian author
     particularly well known for plays that anticipated the Theatre of the
     Absurd, was awarded the Nobel Prize for Literature in 1934; Giovanni
     Verga (1840–1922), Sicilian realist best known for the short story
     'Cavalleria Rusticana'; Giovanni Boccaccio (1313–1375), great Florentine
     writer and poet. A renowned Renaissance humanist, and friend of
     Petrarch, he is particularly well known for the *Decameron*, a frequently
     racy collection of novellas.

10   See *Conversations and Reflections*, pp.194-195, where he also discusses
     his interest in the Etruscans – an important interest that surfaces
     prominently in his late novel *The Gift of a Daughter*.

11   This incident is alluded to, for instance, in the second section of 'S.L.
     i R.S. (An Imagined Greeting)'. (*CP*, 179–180)

12   For detailed discussion of the tangled history of the textual production
     of *A Toy Epic*, see 'Introduction' and 'Afterword', in M. Wynn Thomas
     (ed.), *Emyr Humphreys, A Toy Epic* (Bridgend: Seren, 1989), pp. 7–14
     and 122–50.

13   W. S. Jones (1920–2007). Universally known as 'Wil Sam', he kept a
     garage in Llanystumdwy, near Criccieth, that was the meeting place
     for local writers. He collaborated with Humphreys in the writing and
     producing of *Dinas* (1970), and Humphreys supplied an introduction
     to his collected plays, *Deg Drama Wil Sam* (Capel Garmon: Gwasg
     Carreg Gwalch, 1995).

14   Edmund Wilson (1895–1972) was one of the prominent men of letters
     in the US, his two most influential publications probably being *Axel's
     Castle*, his 1931 study of the Symbolist movement, and *To the Finland
     Station* (1940), which examined the history of European Socialism. He
     was an early champion of Faulkner's work.

15   Martin Esslin (1918–2002) was a Hungarian-born producer and critic,
     educated under Max Reinhardt in Vienna, whose seminal work *The*

Theatre of the Absurd (1961) both gave a name to a new theatrical movement and was immensely influential in its period. He headed BBC Radio Drama from 1963 to 1977, during which time he and his team translated many leading European plays of the time, particularly from the German.

16   John Gwilym Jones (1904–1988) was (alongside Saunders Lewis) the greatest Welsh playwright of the twentieth century, particularly noted for the experimental character of his plays.

2

1   'A Season in Florence', *Wales*, 6 (1946), 120–124.

2   'A Season in Florence', 120. See also his response to a questionnaire, *Wales*, 6 (1946), 27.

3   The best surveys of Saunders Lewis's political, social and cultural ideologies can be found in *Presenting Saunders Lewis*.

4   See, for example, Raymond Williams, *The Country and the City* (London: Chatto and Windus, 1973).

5   Humphreys has always been a huge admirer of Lawrence, whom he first discovered during his schoolboy reading at Rhyl Public Library. As late as 1996 he could still praise Lawrence as a 'poet and a prophet' and as the great writer of a 'vanished England' (*CR*, 225). Slightly earlier he had acclaimed him as 'the last great native English novelist'. (*CR*, 209)

6   This is the period when he published his important early essay 'A Protestant View of the Modern Novel' in *The Listener* (2 April 1953), 557–9: it has been collected in *Conversations and Reflections*, 53–66.

7   'Cymdeithas yr Iaith Gymraeg' was originally a group of young people, mostly college students, that was committed to peaceful direct action to save the language in the aftermath of the dire warning of its imminent demise issued by the elderly Saunders Lewis, in 'Tynged yr Iaith' ('The Fate of the Language'), a famous address broadcast by the BBC in February, 1962. Beginning by campaigning for official status for the language guaranteed by a Welsh-language act, it progressed to agitation for a separate Welsh-language television channel.

8   Labour in Wales had been particularly rattled by the return of Gwynfor Evans (1912–2005), the President of Plaid Cymru, as the MP for Carmarthen in 1966, thus becoming the first Plaid representative to enter Westminster.

9   Many of the central characters in the *Land of the Living* sequence are very loosely modelled on actual prominent figures in the political and

cultural life of the period. Thus, Pen Lewis very broadly resembles the Miners' Union activist (and novelist) Lewis Jones (1897–1937), a Communist with Syndicalist sympathies; John Cilydd brings to mind the similarly tormented figure of E. Prosser Rhys (1901–45), whose homoerotic poem 'Atgof' won the crown at the National Eisteddfod in 1924; there is some similarity between Val Gwyn and William Ambrose Bebb (1894–1955), who came under the influence of leading French cultural figures of the right during his time at the Sorbonne, and became a strongly Europhile nationalist; there are broad parallels between Lord David Iscoed and Lord David Davies of Llandinam, one of the earliest supporters of the League of Nations, while the 'fine country house' of Plas Iscoed is strikingly similar to Gregynog Hall, and Lord Iscoed's two sisters, desirous of turning the Plas into an arts and crafts centre, are obviously based on the two unmarried sisters of Lord Davies who did indeed turn Gregynog into precisely such a venture, complete with a dazzling collection of authentic Impressionist paintings and Rodin sculptures; as for the ineffable 'operator' Sir Prosser Ogmore Pierce, he brings to mind Lloyd George's famous, powerful general factotum, the formidable civil servant Sir Thomas Jones (1870–1955), sometime chairman of Gregynog Press, who succeeded in realising Sir Prosser's dream of an Adult Education College, but based at Harlech and not at Gregynog/ Plas Iscoed. It is important, however, not to (con)fuse these historical figures with fictional creations. As Humphreys has repeatedly emphasised, fiction is 'like a parallel existence . . . the world of fiction always floats a few feet above the actual ground, and enjoys a climate and atmosphere all of its own'. (*CR*, 66)

3

1   He has acknowledged the influence of Kierkegaard on his thinking in this regard. He is a Christian, he has asserted, 'in the sense of taking a Kierkegaardian, existentialist view of the human situation'. (*CR*, 64)
2   Lynette Roberts (1909–95), an arrestingly experimental Welsh Argentinean poet, married to Keidrych Rhys, whose remarkable early poem 'Gods With Stainless Ears' was highly praised by T. S. Eliot; Vernon Watkins (1906–67), a Swansea poet and friend of Dylan Thomas with an international reputation during his lifetime; R. Williams Parry (1884–1956), one of the greatest poets of the twentieth-century Welsh-language literary Renaissance.
3   Saunders Lewis, 'Cenedlaetholdeb a Chyfalaf', in *Canlyn Arthur* (1938; Llandysul: Gwasg Gomer, 1985), 20.

4   The phrase 'a daily plebiscite' occurs in the Breton Ernest Renan's famous and influential essay, 'Qu'est-ce qu'une nation?', ('What is a Nation?'), a lecture delivered at the Sorbonne in 1882. For an English version see Geoff Eley and Ronald Grigor Suny (eds), *Becoming National: a Reader* (Oxford: Oxford University Press, 1996), 41–55.

5   In 'The Pleasure of the Text' (1973) Roland Barthes coined the term 'white writing' ('*écriture blanche*') to describe a 'neutral' style, free of ideological biases.

6   'J.S.L.', in Joseph Clancy (trans.), *Twentieth-Century Welsh Poems* (Llandysul: Gomer Press, 1982), 54–55. The next lines in the sonnet read 'You were a fool, O forsaken one, a fool; for woe / To a bird without kin, and a peerless soul without backing.' The concept of the heroic 'fool' – one who, with a kind of sublime innocence, lives out a religious or political ideal in a disconcertingly 'pure' way and to an extreme conclusion that scandalises and angers established society – is a recurrent one in Humphreys's fiction.

7   Emyr Humphreys, *Theatr Saunders Lewis* (Astudiaethau Theatr Cymru, Rhif 1, Bangor, 1979).

8   The episode is loosely analogous to that involving the two young protesters against the 1969 Royal Investiture who were accidentally killed when the bomb they placed outside government offices in Abergele exploded.

4

1   Lewis Valentine (1893–1986) was a pacifist minister and author who (like John Cilydd) served in the Royal Army Medical Corps in the First World War. Between 1969 and 1972 he published his war memoirs under the title *Dyddiadur Milwr* in the Baptist periodical *Seren Gomer* and this became an important source for Humphreys when he was embarking on his *Land of the Living* sequence. D. J. Williams (1885–1970) was a teacher and noted author of two classic rural memoirs, *Hen Dŷ Ffarm* (1953) and *Yn Chwech ar Hugain Oed* (1959). Both Williams and Valentine were founder members of Plaid Cymru in 1925, and the latter served as the party's first President.

2   See D. J. Taylor, *After the War: the Novel and England since 1984* (London: Flamingo, 1994); Brian W. Shaffer (ed.), *A Companion to the British and Irish Novel, 1945–2000* (London: Palgrave Macmillan, 2007); Marina MacKay and Lyndsey Stonebridge (eds), *British Fiction after Modernism: the Novel at Mid-Century* (London: Palgrave Macmillan, 2007).

3 'Introduction: Faulkner: Past and Present', in Robert Penn Warren (ed.), *Faulkner: A Collection of Critical Essays* (Englewood Cliffs, NJ: Prentiss-Hall, 1966), p. 5.

4 See Cleanth Brooks, *William Faulkner: The Yoknapatawpha Country* (New Haven: Yale University Press, 1966).

5 Daniel Owen (1836–95), from Mold, Flintshire, published several notable works of fiction, the most famous being *Rhys Lewis* (1885), *Enoc Huws* (1891) and *Gwen Tomos* (1894); E. Tegla Davies (1880–1967) was a Wesleyan Methodist minister who wrote pioneering children's fiction (*Hunangofiant Tomi*, 1912; *Nedw*, 1922) as well as the important historical novel *Gŵr Pen y Bryn* (1923); daughter of a North Wales quarryman, Kate Roberts was a fine novelist and a major short-story writer. Humphreys expressed his enormous admiration for her work in the 1988 essay 'Under the Yoke' (an allusion to her important novel *Traed Mewn Cyffion*), as well as in Channel Four drama-documentaries that led subsequently to the publication *The Triple Net: Kate Roberts and Her Friends* (London: Channel Four Publications, 1988).

6 *Under Milk Wood* was first broadcast on the Third Programme on 25 January 1954, after Dylan Thomas's death the previous November, with Richard Burton as First Voice.

7 *The Times*, November 1958.

8 It was Walter Todd, a fellow producer at the BBC in the late 1950s, who introduced him to Wittgenstein's work. '"The world is that which is the case"; "It's not how a thing is but why it is" – all these aphorisms reverberated in my mind and led me to feel that this was a valid way of writing fiction in one language about a life that had happened for the most part in another.' (*CR*, 136)

9 *The New Statesman*, 1958.

10 What Michael recalls are the famous lines expressing love of country (specifically Gwynedd), which he quotes from memory: 'I love her marshlands and her mountains / Her forts near her woods, her comely domains / Her valleys, her meadowlands, and her fountains, / Her white seagulls, and gracious women.' (*TT*, 96–7) Hywel ap Owain Gwynedd (fl. 1140–70), illegitimate son of Owain Gwynedd, one of the most powerful of medieval Welsh princes, was an accomplished poet.

11 Milan Kundera, *The Book of Laughter and Forgetting* (1980).

12 Repeated from a private conversation I had with Emyr Humphreys.

13 For a character of similarly enigmatic moral character see Graham Greene, *Monsignor Quixote* (London: Bodley Head, 1982).

14   Hywel Dda (*d*. 949 or 950), ordered the native laws of Wales to be codified at his court at Whitland, Dyfed. This system of laws remained in force until the Act of Union of England and Wales in 1536.

15   Having begun *Blodeuwedd* in the 1920s, Saunders Lewis completed it in 1948. The play is based on the celebrated story in the *Mabinogion* about a woman who is fashioned out of flowers by the wizard Gwydion as wife for Lleu Llawgyffes, a prince cursed by the witch Arianrhod never to win the hand of a mortal woman. Disaster strikes when Blodeuwedd begins a passionate affair with a passing prince, Gronw Pebr. Her punishment for this is to be turned by Gwydion into an owl and to be confined to fly only by night. During the second half of the twentieth century, a number of Welsh women writers, including Gillian Clarke, have memorably revisited the story and narrated it anew from Blodeuwedd's perspective.

16   Georg Lukács, *The Historical Novel* (London: Merlin, 1962).

17   T. Gwynn Jones (1871–1949) was the pre-eminent strict-metre poet of the twentieth century, and the greatest since the golden age of such poetry in the late medieval period. Written in 1926–6, his powerful 'awdl' 'Argoed' tells the story of a poet of ancient Gaul who, having visited the seat of Imperial Roman power and realised it is intent on obliterating his culture, sentences himself to permanent exile just before his tribe sets fire to its stronghold in an act of self-immolation rather than be conquered by the Romans. 'Argoed' was also the name of the coal mine where two of the novelist Daniel Owen's brothers were drowned.

5

1   Richard Wilbur, 'Clearness', *The Poems of Richard Wilbur* (New York and London: Harcourt Brace Jovanovich, 1963), p. 145.

2   A colourful and controversial figure, the debonair Goronwy Rees (1909–1979), academic, journalist and author, became Assistant Editor of the *Spectator* in 1936. More than half a century after their first encounter, Humphreys was to view Rees with a mixture of admiration and censure. By then, he saw him as the diametric opposite to Saunders Lewis: 'Each of them followed his own path, which in Goronwy Rees's case led to All Souls, and in Saunders Lewis's case led to Wormwood Scrubs. To me this seems the prototypical situation.' (*CR*, 132)

3   Along with the poet of the 'Gododdin', Aneirin (later sixth-century), Taliesin (also later sixth-century) was the founder of the strict-metre tradition and a poet of the 'Old North' – the region roughly between

Sterling and the Humber estuary that continued to be the homeland of some of the 'Brythonic' people (eventually to become the Welsh) even after the early incursions of the Angles and the Saxons.

4   *Poems of Richard Wilbur*, p. 72.

5   Taliesin the wizard figures in the medieval text *Hanes Taliesin*, which draws on folktale. The story concerns the witch Ceridwen who brews a magic potion in her cauldron, intending to bestow on her dullard son Morfran the gift of poetry. She sets her servant, Gwion Bach, to stir the cauldron, and in so doing a drop of the potion drops into his mouth, instantly endowing him with magic powers. Incensed, Ceridwen pursues him in a variety of shapes, but each time Gwion is able to conjure up a further metamorphic change that enables him to elude her until, eventually, he is swallowed by the witch when he adopts the form of a grain of wheat and she that of a chicken. Nine months later she gives birth to a son who is so beautiful that she cannot bring herself to kill him. Instead, she sets him adrift at sea, and the baby makes landfall in the realm of Elffin ap Gwyddno Garanhir, who names him 'Taliesin', 'beautiful of brow'. Upon attaining manhood, he is taken by Elffin to the great court of Maelgwn Gwynedd, and there he astonishes the assembled magi with his remarkable magical prowess.

6   Probably a monk, Geoffrey of Monmouth (1090–1155) is best known for his *Historia Regum Britanniae*, a pseudo-history that purports to record the pedigree and history of the 'kings of Britain' from the very beginning. It includes accounts of the magician Myrddin/ Merlin and lays the foundations for all the later romances about the court of King Arthur. *Pedair Cainc y Mabinogi* (rendered as *The Mabinogion* in Charlotte Guest's immensely influential nineteenth-century English redaction) is a collection of wonderful and fantastic stories recorded by an anonymous monk in the late medieval period. Humphreys draws a seminal distinction between Geoffrey's production (which he sees as involving the 'capture' by an invading culture of indigenous Welsh materials that subsequently became the means of cultural subordination and marginalisation, as happened most conspicuously in the case of the later Arthurian literature) and an authentic native story of legendary matter that has continued to be used to reinforce and enrich Welsh cultural practice.

7   John Dee (1527–1608) was the star magus of the Elizabethan age, reputed to possess magical powers. He became consultant to Queen Elizabeth and in 1576 worked on manuscripts (now lost) outlining his blueprint for a British Empire based on the imaginary exploits of King Arthur, whom he credited with extensive Continental conquests, and

on the legend of Prince Madoc, who had crossed the Atlantic and thus first 'discovered' America.

8   Ieuan Brydydd Hir (Evan Evans, 1731–88), was a poor Anglican curate, much given to angry despair and drink, who tramped the country tirelessly in search of what remained in manuscript form, in the fusty attics of great country houses, of the Welsh poetic treasures of the great late medieval period and earlier. William Williams Pantycelyn (1717–91) was the greatest of restlessly peripatetic Welsh Methodist evangelists and a poet who devoted his genius primarily to writing a huge number of great hymns that have continued to haunt the Welsh mind. Iolo Morganwg (1747–1826) was one of the most colourful and singular figures ever to have been produced by Wales, and an inspired mythographer of his people. He was a self-educated stonemason who became a maverick antiquary and was a Unitarian, a Freemason, and Radical. A confirmed laudanum taker he manufactured fake poems by Dafydd ap Gwilym and also a fake history of the Welsh that, in the accepted eighteenth-century fashion, traced their origins back to ancient Druidic times. And out of this inspired farrago of nonsense he not only conjured the concept of a mystic brotherhood of contemporary poets who were the direct heirs of the Ancient Druids but also turned that concept into a bizarre modern reality when he convened the first meeting of what he called a modern Gorsedd of the Bards of Ancient Britain, a ritual that is still followed annually at the National Eisteddfod.

9   William Price (1800–1903), a militant Chartist from Pontypridd often credited with reviving the ancient practice of cremation, was notorious for his scandalous practices and progressive beliefs – they included free love and vegetarianism and a virulent hatred of iron masters, orthodox religion and vivisection.

6

1   The actions of the Chetnik group within the Yugoslav army during the Second World War remain controversial – not least their policy of selective collaboration with the enemy and their terrorist actions against the Croats, Muslims and Partisans in the interests of establishing a Greater Serbia.

Select Bibliography

Fiction, Poems and Critical Writings
(Details listed are those of the texts on first publication. A fuller
bibliography of Humphreys's writings is available in Green,
*Emyr Humphreys: A Postcolonial Novelist?***)**

The Little Kingdom (London: Eyre and Spottiswoode, 1946).
The Voice of a Stranger (London: Eyre and Spottiswoode, 1949).
A Change of Heart (London: Eyre and Spottiswoode, 1951).
Hear and Forgive (London: Macdonald, 1952).
A Man's Estate (London: Victor Gollancz, 1955).
The Italian Wife (London: Eyre and Spottiswoode, 1957).
Y Tri Llais (Llandybie: Llyfrau'r Dryw, 1958).
A Toy Epic (London: Eyre and Spottiswoode, 1958).
The Gift (London: Eyre and Spottiswoode, 1963).
Outside the House of Baal (London: Hodder and Stoughton, 1965).
Natives (London: Secker and Warburg, 1968).
National Winner (London: Macdonald, 1971).
Flesh and Blood (London: Hodder and Stoughton, 1974).
The Best of Friends (London: Hodder and Stoughton, 1978).
The Anchor Tree (London: Hodder and Stoughton, 1980).
The Taliesin Tradition (Bury St Edmunds: Black Raven Press, 1983).
Jones (London: Dent, 1984).
Salt of the Earth (London: Dent, 1985).
An Absolute Hero (London: Dent, 1986).
Darn o Dir [translation by W. J. Jones of *A Little Kingdom*] (Penygroes:
      Gwasg Gwynedd. 1986).
Open Secrets (London: Dent, 1988).

Bonds of Attachment (London: Macdonald, 1991).

Unconditional Surrender (Bridgend: Seren, 1996).

The Gift of a Daughter (Bridgend: Seren, 1998).

Collected Poems (Cardiff: University of Wales Press, 1999).

Dal Pen Rheswm (Caerdydd: Gwasg Prifysgol Cymru, 1999).

Ghosts and Strangers (Bridgend: Seren, 2001).

Conversations and Reflections (Cardiff: University of Wales Press, 2002).

Old People are a Problem (Bridgend: Seren, 2003).

The Shop (Bridgend: Seren, 2005).

The Woman at the Window (Bridgend: Seren, 2009).

Shards of Light (Cardiff: University of Wales Press, 2018).

Secondary texts
(Reviews of Humphreys's work are listed in Green, *Emyr Humphreys: A Postcolonial Novelist?*)

Bohata, Kirsti, *Postcolonialism Revisited* (Cardiff: University of Wales Press, 2004).

Ellis, Sylvia, '*Ancestor Worship* and other geographies: a pattern in the poetry of Emyr Humphreys', *Welsh Writing in English: a Yearbook of Critical Essays*, 6 (2000), 163–74.

Gramich, Katie, 'God, word and nation: language and religion in works by V. S. Naipaul, Edna O'Brien and Emyr Humphreys', in James A. Davies (ed.), *Writing Region and Nation 4* (Swansea: University College of Swansea, 1994), pp. 229–41.

— 'Both in and out of the Game', in M. Wynn Thomas (ed.), *Writing Wales in English* (Cardiff: University of Wales Press, 2003), pp. 255–277.

Green, Diane, 'From pig-sty to Benin head: modernism and postcolonialism in Emyr Humphreys's *Jones*', *Welsh Writing in English: a Yearbook of Critical Essays*, 7 (2001-2002), 35–49.

— 'The Blodeuwedd myth and the dysfunctional family unit in Emyr Humphreys's novels', *Revista Alicantina de Estudios Ingleses (RAEI)*, (November, 2003), 129–46.

— '"The first interpreter": Emyr Humphreys's use of titles and epigraphs', *Welsh Writing in English*, 10 (2005), 98–120.

— *Emyr Humphreys: A Postcolonial Novelist?* (Cardiff: University of Wales Press, 2009).

Hooker, Jeremy, *The Poetry of Place* (Manchester: Carcanet, 1982).

— *Imagining Wales: A View of Modern Welsh Writing in English* (Cardiff: University of Wales Press, 2001).

Jones, John Gwilym, 'Dawn Emyr Humphreys', *Yr Arloeswr Newydd*, 1 (1959), 17–18.

Lewis, Saunders, 'Athens and Bethel', *Western Mail*, 28 October 1955.

Knight, Stephen, *A Hundred Years of Fiction* (Cardiff: University of Wales Press, 2003).

Lloyd, Vernon, 'Variations on a theme by Aeschylus', *Anglo-Welsh Review*, 73 (1983), 49–63.

Mathias, Roland, *A Ride Through the Wood* (Bridgend: Poetry Wales Press, 1985).

Morgan, Andre, 'Three Voices', *Planet*, 39 (1977), 44–9.

Morgan, Derec Llwyd, 'Emyr Humphreys: Llenor y Llwyth', *Ysgrifau Beirniadol*, VII (1971), 285–303.

Peach, Linden, 'The Woolf at Faulkner's door; modernism and the body in Emyr Humphreys's 1950s fiction', *Welsh Writing in English: A Yearbook of Critical Essays*, 6 (2000), 144–62.

—, *The Fiction of Emyr Humphreys: Contemporary Critical Perspectives* (Cardiff: University of Wales Press, 2011).

Pikoulis, John, 'The Wounded Bard', *New Welsh Review*, 26 (1994), 22–34.

Thomas, Karen, 'Cloffi Rhwng Dau Feddwl', *Barn* (Ebrill, 1983).

Thomas, M. Wynn, *Emyr Humphreys* (Caernarfon; Gwasg Pantycelyn, 1989).

— 'Hanes Dwy Chwaer: olrhain hanes *Y Tri Llais*', *Barn* (Ionawr ac Ebrill, 1989), 23–5.

— 'The poetry of Emyr Humphreys', *Poetry Wales*, 25: 2 (1989), 10–12.

— 'Emyr Humphreys: Mythic Realist', in J.J. Simon and Alain Giuev (eds), *English Studies III* (Luxembourg: Centre Universitat de Luxembourg, 1991), 264–81.

— 'The Relentlessness of Emyr Humphreys', *New Welsh Review*, 13 (1991), 37–40.

— *Internal Difference: Twentieth-Century Writing in Wales* (Cardiff: University of Wales Press, 1992).

— 'Emyr Humphreys, Regional Novelist?', in K. D. M. Snell (ed.), *The Regional Novel in Britain and Ireland* (Cambridge: Cambridge University Press, 1998), pp. 201–20.

— 'Emyr Humphreys: y sgrifennwr ar y mur', *Golwg*, 234 (1998), 18–19.

— *In the Shadow of the Pulpit: Literature and Nonconformist Wales* (Cardiff: University of Wales Press, 2010).

— *All That is Wales* (Cardiff: University of Wales Press, 2017).

Wiliams, Gerwyn, 'Options and Allegiances', *Planet*, 71 (1988), 30–6.

Williams, Ioan, *Emyr Humphreys* (Cardiff: University of Wales Press, 1980).

— 'The land of the living', *Planet*, 52 (1985), 97–105.

Williams, Raymond, *Who Speaks for Wales? Nation, Culture, Identity*, ed. Daniel G. Williams (Cardiff: University of Wales Press, 2003).

INDEX